Viola Martinez, California Paiute

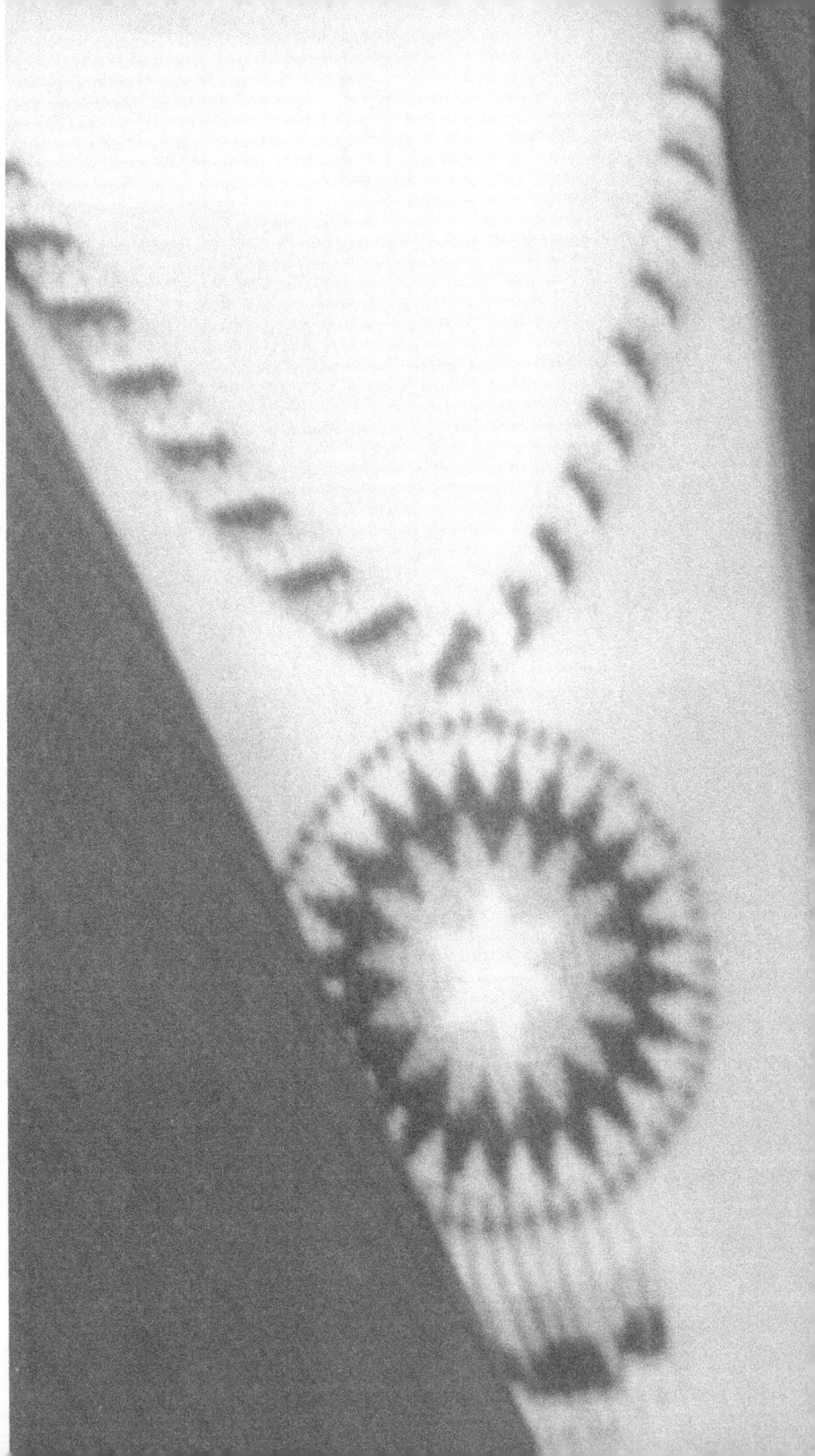

Viola Martinez, California Paiute

Living in Two Worlds

Diana Meyers Bahr

University of Oklahoma Press • Norman

Also by Diana Meyers Bahr

From Mission to Metropolis: Cupeño Indian Women in Los Angeles (Norman, 1993)

This book is published with the generous assistance of Edith Kinney Gaylord.

LIBRARY OF CONGRESS CATALOGING-IN-PUBLICATION DATA

Bahr, Diana Meyers, 1930–
    Viola Martinez, California Paiute: living in two worlds /
Diana Meyers Bahr.
        p. cm.
    Includes bibliographical references and index.
    ISBN 978-0-8061-4159-6 (paper)
    1. Martinez, Viola M. (Viola Meroney).   2. Paiute Indians—
Biography.   3. Indian women—United States.   I. Title.

E99.P2 M383 2003
979.4004'9745—DC21
[B]   2002074040

The paper in this book meets the guidelines for permanence and durability of the Committee on Production Guidelines for Book Longevity of the Council on Library Resources, Inc. ∞

Contents

Illustrations

Acknowledgments

MY GRATEFUL APPRECIATION IS EXTENDED TO LINDA STOWE for her remarkable transcribing and her personal interest in Vi's story. I wish to thank Kenneth Wade, Librarian, UCLA American Indian Studies Center, for his diligence in researching answers to my abstruse questions regarding Indian affairs in general and Owens Valley Paiutes, specifically. The responses regarding demographics of American Indians in Los Angeles by Michael McLaughlin, Librarian, American Indian Resource Center, Huntington Park, California, were impressively prompt and exact. Professor Carole Goldberg, UCLA School of Law, provided concise and invaluable information regarding involuntary termination of parental rights of Indian people. I extend my appreciation to Jeannine Gendar for swiftly and graciously granting permission to include in this book the portion of chapter 8 that had previously been published in *News from Native California*. To Barbara Siegemund-Broka I say here what I have said to many others about her: I am fortunate indeed to have had an editor who is so conscientious and discerning. I have relied with complete confidence on Sue Kunitomi Embrey, chairperson of the Manzanar Committee, to keep me current on the Manzanar Historic Site, particularly on the contested wording of the commemorative plaques.

When I have needed a sympathetic listener I have turned to my husband Ehrhard (Ted) Bahr. Without fail, he has responded with sensitive and perceptive insights. My deepest appreciation goes to Viola Meroney Martinez and her extended family for sharing with me recollections gleaned not only from their memories but also from their hearts.

Viola Martinez, California Paiute

Introduction
The Marginal Person

WE MET AT A CHINESE-VIETNAMESE WEDDING. I, a white woman, a native of Los Angeles, am related to the bride, Rosanne Nguyen Hong, through the marriage of my son, Timothy John Meyers, to the bride's sister, Jackie Nguyen Meyers. Viola Meroney Martinez and her family have been friends for more than twenty years with the bride's parents, Thien and Dung Nguyen. When Bobbie Keener, a guest who was close to both the Nguyen family and Viola, learned that I write about American Indian women, she said, "You should write Vi's story." I was intrigued from that moment, but Vi was cautious. I pursued the idea of our working together for more than a year before I convinced her to relate her life story.

After we had been working on our project for several months, Vi visited my class on oral histories of American Indian women at the University of California at Los Angeles (UCLA). Responding to a question from a student, she divulged that she had agreed to work with me for three reasons: first, I was persistent; second, I had written about American Indian women in a previous book; and third, and most important, she had come to consider me as kin because of our mutual connections with the Nguyen family.

Our collaboration was intended to allow Viola Meroney Martinez to tell her own remarkable story, spanning nine decades of the twentieth century. Viola is, however, diffident, often questioning, "What makes me think my story is so important?" She is also very sensitive about not appearing as though she knows more than her Paiute family and friends in regard to the events she narrates. She asked that this statement be included early in the book: "These are not just my childhood memories but also recollections of what people have told me. My memory may not be completely accurate, and others may recall events differently; but I am telling the story to the best of my recollection."

During the time Vi and I were working together, I was also interviewing Leonard Freedman, professor emeritus of political science at UCLA. I am grateful to Dr. Freedman for planting the seed that grew into the argument presented in this book. While we were working on his life history, he advised, "Look upon the margin not as a place where you are squeezed, where you are just a bridge to be walked over, to be trampled on, but, rather as the most interesting place to be, the most creative place to be." He then qualified his assertion: "The margin is an opportunity for *some* people. You have to have a certain hardihood to be able to take the lumps."[1]

As Viola's life story took shape for me during sixteen months of interviews with eight individuals, I realized that she exemplifies Freedman's distinctive perspective on marginality. In contrast to Freedman's positive perception, marginality historically has been perceived as a negative status. Marginal persons, as defined by sociologist Everett V. Stonequist in 1937, are "condemned to live in two societies and in two, not merely different, but antagonistic cultures." The marginal person "is poised in psychological uncertainty between two (or more) social worlds."[2] Although Stonequist himself acknowledged that the marginal person could become the individual with the wider horizon, the negative connotation has persisted for more than sixty years.

Stonequist's theory of marginality has been discarded within the last decade as a viable model, yet the metaphor of being "suspended between cultures" has retained remarkable vitality. It is still used, for example, to characterize the experience of Indian children in boarding schools.[3] Hazel W. Hertzberg in *The Search for an American Indian Identity* describes Indian boarding school graduates: "They lived in two, or three worlds, and most of them were not quite comfortable in any."[4]

Marginality as a negative concept involves ethnocentrism, nurtured, in part, by reliance on written sources. Many scholars have thought of oral accounts as peripheral, if they have considered them at all.[5] Within the last decade, however, scholars have explored a new possibility: that boarding school students might have responded to white education in individualistic, syncretistic ways. This research has relied heavily on Indian oral accounts. Emerging in the literature is awareness that perhaps not all of these students were passive recipients of white assimilation.[6]

Considering only marginality's negative aspects, one could easily assume that Viola Martinez would find herself "poised in psychological uncertainty." She did find herself, after several years at Sherman Institute Federal Indian Boarding School in Riverside, California, on the margins of two cultures, Paiute and white. At Sherman Institute she realized almost immediately that language was a critical issue. Her "outing" experience—being sent to work for a white family—was initially demoralizing. She returned home to California's Owens Valley only once in twelve years, and that trip was a tragic one. The loss of her native language and other assaults on her identity could easily have fulfilled Stonequist's criteria for marginality. Her narration, however, provides deeper insight into the margin in which Viola found herself and presents an opportunity for reinterpreting, rather than discarding, the concept of marginality. Her narrative indicates that she, in Freedman's terms, was able to look upon the margin, not as confinement, but as an opportunity to grow, if she were creative.

What characterizes such growth? More than thirty years ago Malcolm McFee found that "a man is more than a culture container," and that acculturation can supplement as well as replace. He called the Blackfeet in his study "150 percent men."[7] In support of McFee's model a study of "culturally marginal" individuals conducted in 1989 by James A. Clifton and multidisciplinary colleagues established that such people become "not diminished, but culturally enlarged."[8]

What is the process by which an individual becomes "culturally enlarged"? Jane Katz offers insight into the complexity of this process in her introduction to *Messengers of the Wind: Native American Women Tell Their Life Stories*. "Some . . . come to see traditions as living and breathing entities that can be molded to fit times. Nevertheless, many Native Americans have been torn apart by value and identity conflicts."[9] Viola Martinez has experienced both responses and in reconciling them, has expanded the margins of her existence. Despite complex, often painful reassessments, she has learned to embrace new ways without abandoning the old.

This process begins with imagination. N. Scott Momaday, a Kiowa, elegantly expresses the significance of imagination in "A Man Made of Words": "We are what we imagine. Our very existence consists of our imagination of ourselves. The greatest tragedy that can befall us is to go unimagined."[10]

To borrow Clifton's fitting image, I intend to "[use] biography as a magnifying glass."[11] In this book I have attempted to illuminate how Viola has imagined herself. Her imagining began with a profound question: "How come my brain is different from a white person's brain?" The question led to a resolve: "I was going to prove myself to those people who thought my brain was different because I was brown and they were white."[12]

This resolve required her to confront the issue of race. Although legal scholar Kenneth L. Karst, in discussing legal aspects of identity, argues that race is a myth, he cautions, "one danger in recognizing the mythical quality of [racial] identities is that we may ignore the myths' momentous effect on the lives of real people."[13] Viola was unquestionably affected by the myth of white superiority while she attended Sherman Institute. "I was always trying to see ways where I could be very much like white girls," she says, "because they were the ones who were going places, becoming teachers, or doing different things."[14]

Viola's daughter, Vianne Martinez Wentzell, experienced the myth of race differently than did her mother. When she visited Owens Valley, she sometimes was harassed by Paiute children. "I think [they] thought I didn't belong there," she relates, "because I was from Los Angeles, and I am fair [complexioned], and they probably thought I was not Indian."[15]

Paula Gunn Allen, a Laguna Pueblo, has written frequently about this dilemma. "The subject of Indianness generates intense response . . . when belonging is a central value." She contends that, although Indian people are classified according to their "Indianness," no one knows what the "qualifying characteristics" are.[16]

Who is an Indian? While stereotypes, complexities, and ambiguities cannot be ignored, Indianness has been defined in six basic ways: (1) legal definitions, primarily enrollment in a tribe that is recognized by the federal government; (2) self-declaration, used formally by the U.S. Bureau of the Census and informally in exchanges with both Indian and white segments of the population; (3) recognition by an Indian community; (4) recognition by non-Indians; (5) biological definition, usually specified by blood quantum; and (6) cultural definitions, as perceived by both Indians and whites. [17]

Legal definition. Enrollment in the Bishop Band of Owens Valley Paiute is of critical significance to Viola and her family because it preserves their legal status within the Paiute community and allows Viola to maintain her land allotment on the Paiute Indian Reservation in Bishop, California.

Self-definition is a constant with Viola and her children. They identify themselves as Owens Valley Paiute whenever the identification is appropriate, as with the Census Bureau.

Recognition by the Indian community. Although Viola experienced a certain estrangement upon her initial return to Owens Valley, recognition by the Paiute community also has been a constant, as evidenced by the deeply rooted memories of her children, Kirkland Robert Martinez and Vianne.

Recognition by the non-Indian community. Although Viola is most often assumed to be Mexican American because of the surname Martinez, she quickly and positively corrects the assumption. She feels keenly a responsibility to acknowledge her Indianness and to mediate between white and Indian societies. Because of her physical appearance, Vianne is rarely perceived as Indian, a misperception she corrects if she believes it fitting, as with coworkers and neighbors. Kirk says that it is important to him that people in the city know he is Indian, and he makes an effort to assert this identity.

Biological definition. When asked about blood quantum as a criterion for identifying Indianness, Vi recalls the passionate objections made by her aunt Mary Ann Brazzanovich when white people asked her how she was related to certain individuals: "That is not important. We don't care about that. We love and take care of each other. We *all* belong." In regard to the blood quantum issue in Owens Valley today, Vi says, "It is not even discussed. There is no way for an individual to prove how much Indian blood he or she has. We don't even mention it."

Cultural definitions are of primary importance to Viola and her family and, despite their urban lifestyle, permeate their self-perceptions. Viola, especially, exemplifies the model presented by Karst: "Not 'assimilation' in the sense of an identity lost, but integration in the sense of a reality renamed, an identity renewed."[18]

♦ ♦ ♦

Issues raised in chapters 1, 3, 4, and 7 warrant consideration here. Chapter 1, "Facing the Sunrise: Owens Valley," presents two salient factors: contact with whites occurred in Owens Valley relatively late in the history of Indian-white relations; within ten years of this contact the Paiutes' centuries-old lifestyle was virtually destroyed.

Before contact with whites, the Paiutes traditionally subsisted on the seasonal harvest of irrigated wild plants, seeds, and root crops, supplemented by insects, small game, fish, deer, mountain sheep, waterfowl, jackrabbits, and the highly valued acorns and pine nuts (piñons). Because of cattle grazing and the fencing of ranches on their land, the Paiutes no longer had access to water sources, nor to the vegetation that they had previously harvested. Within a decade of contact, Owens Valley Paiute were forced into wage labor, resulting in total dependence on white-owned ranches and in an erosion of traditional Paiute lifestyle.

Although historians agree that Spanish explorers may have entered the Owens Valley in the early 1800s, no records of these encounters have been found. The Old Spanish Trail traversed by the Franciscan missionaries ran considerably south of the valley, but Paiutes most likely had some contact with travelers, as evidenced by their rudimentary knowledge of Spanish.[19] However, for three hundred years after Juan Rodríguez Cabrillo arrived in California in 1542, the Paiutes lived undisturbed by white intrusion. Once contact had been made, in the 1840s, continuing friction was fueled by conflicts between traditional Paiute subsistence and white settlement.

The Indian "war" between 1862 and 1865 that made life for both Indians and whites in Owens Valley daunting and unpredictable is characterized in all accounts as inevitable.[20] The immediate cause of the conflict was the killing by Paiutes of cattle for food, during the relentlessly severe winter of 1861–62. Extensive cattle grazing destroyed the seed plants; and lumbering, which had increased in Owens Valley as a consequence of mining, depleted piñon trees, exhausting essential food sources for the Native peoples. When Paiutes, in order to survive, began killing cattle in the valley, whites retaliated by killing Paiutes.

Indians from other areas, including Kern and Tulare, joined forces with the Paiutes under several leaders, notably Captain George of the southern Owens Valley and Joaquin Jim, Yokuts from the north. Although the Paiutes had not been hostile, they had nevertheless been under surveillance by the U.S. Army and the Office of Indian Affairs. In 1859, some 22,300 acres near Independence, California, in the southern Owens Valley had been set aside as a possible reserve for the indigenous people of the area.[21] During the same year Capt. John W. Davidson had led an expedition to explore the region. Davidson wrote about the Native people, "Their character is that of an interesting, peaceful, industrious people, deserving the protection and watchful care of the government."[22]

By the end of April 1862, these "peaceful, industrious" Indians were so fully engaged in hostilities that they were in undisputed control of Owens Valley.[23] The U.S. Army responded in June with a force of two hundred men under the command of Col. George S. Evans. After destroying Paiute food caches, Evans established Camp Independence on 4 July 1862. As the armed conflict extended into 1863, the military used increasingly ruthless tactics. Capt. Moses A. McLaughlin took command of Fort Independence in April. McLaughlin, employing a "scorched earth" strategy, subdued the Paiute, four hundred of whom surrendered at Camp Independence in June 1863. Hungry and despondent, six hundred others soon followed.

The one thousand Indians who had surrendered were forced to march 175 miles south to the San Sebastian Reservation near Fort Tejon in the Tehachapi Mountains. Over one hundred and fifty died or escaped during the march. Hundreds more escaped when it became clear that Fort Tejon was not equipped to hold them in internment, nor was the reservation prepared to provide adequate food and clothing. Intermittent hostilities between whites and Indians continued until the end of 1865, with the death of Joaquin Jim. Although most of the dislocated Paiutes gradually made their way back to Owens Valley, their traditional existence had been effectively destroyed. They found themselves primarily dependent on whites for subsistence.

Chapter 3, "Far from Home: Sherman Institute Boarding School," presents evidence of a growing body of scholarly literature on federal Indian boarding schools. Scholars have recently recognized that repeated negative descriptions of the boarding schools have flattened the discourse on students' complex responses. New scholarship stresses the interpretation of individual experiences.

Individual experiences in boarding school invariably included exposure to white religion. Scholars have recognized that a religious middle ground often proved to be the site of provocative and complex negotiations in the construction of identity. Gretchen M. Bataille and Kathleen M. Sands point out that Anna Moore Shaw's adjustment to boarding school may have been facilitated by her family's participation in Christian practices, "which may have created a neutral ground to bridge the disparities in experiences."[24]

Hertzberg argues that boarding school education exposed students to influential ideas and images that they used in defining themselves as Indians and in interactions with whites. "Of these, probably the most important was Christianity, as refracted through the Indian schools, the various denomination missions, and the Christian reform organizations."[25]

Mary Young points out that conversion to Christianity required Indians to accept intellectual abstractions as well as psychological distancing, both of which were alien to the Indian individual's sense of self in relation to others. "At the same time, however, popular Christianity contained many of the magical and ceremonial elements—and metaphysical assumptions—common to Native American religions."[26]

What the literature on Indian boarding schools failed to take into account until the late 1980s and 1990s was the individual response. David Wallace Adams points out that policymakers did not expect Indian children to be active in their own acculturation. "Presumably, the self-evident superiority of white civilization together with the malleability of youth, were sufficient to guarantee the children's cooperation.... [However] not only did some students continuously exhibit patterns of resistance, but even those who cooperated often did so on their own terms."[27] As Viola's narrative unfolds, evidence mounts that conveys her determination to respond to boarding school on her own terms.

In chapter 4, "The Creative Margin," Viola articulates the ways in which her experiences are both similar to and different from those of other Indian students in boarding schools. In the introduction to *First Person, First Peoples: Native American Graduates Tell Their Stories*, Andrew Garrod and Colleen Larimore discuss the image of Native American students trying to walk between two worlds. "This metaphor implies that in order to survive and participate successfully in mainstream cultures, Native American students must learn an alien way to walk, talk, think, and act.... This expectation places the burden of assimilation squarely on the shoulders of Native American students and can be ... brutalizing to one's identity and spirituality."[28] Recognizing that the burden was on her shoulders, Viola reiterates in her narrative that she "had a brain" and what she did with it was up to her. Viola's story attests to her ability to triumph over assaults on her identity by walking creatively in both worlds.

In doing so, Viola contradicts a particular stereotype of American Indians, described here by Elizabeth Cook-Lynn, a Crow Creek Sioux: "There is no image of an American Indian intellectual. . . . It is as though the American Indian has no intellectual voice with which to enter into America's important dialogues. . . . It is as though the American Indian does not exist except in *faux* history or corrupt myth."[29] Margot Liberty argues, "Indian intellectuals are in most cases the product of an extensive interplay between Indian and non-Indian life."[30] Viola's success at mastering the interplay between her Indian life in rural Owens Valley and her non-Indian life in urban Los Angeles has earned her high regard in both communities as an intellectual Indian elder.

Chapter 7, "Expanded Margins: Urban Opportunities," relies on the scholarly literature regarding urbanization of Indian people, particularly the federal government's policy of Termination and Relocation. The documents of the Los Angeles Native American Ministry have proven to be invaluable in documenting Viola's participation in the founding of this urban ministry.

Terry Straus and Debra Valentino, both of whom work in the Chicago Indian community, argue, "Urban is not a *kind* of Indian. It is a kind of experience."[31] While it is difficult not to regard as urban those people, Indian or non-Indian, who live, work, and raise their families in the city, I did find it constructive to examine Viola's experiences and those of her family apart from the urban-rural categorization.

In 1953 the House of Representatives passed House Concurrent Resolution 108 (Eighty-third Congress, first session), which called for the termination of federal controls over all Indians in California, Florida, Iowa, New York, and Texas, in addition to six other specific tribes elsewhere in the United States. William A. Brophy, commissioner of Indian affairs in 1947, believed that trust status had "hindered" California Indians, who were considered to be "progressive American Citizens" and campaigned for termination of California tribes.[32] President Dwight Eisenhower, in signing the bills, expressed concern that there was no requirement that the Indians be consulted and urged Congress to amend the bill to provide for such consultation. However, termination was extended to a great number of other tribes in 1954 without consultation. Finally, in 1958, Secretary of the Interior Fred A. Seaton announced that no further termination action would be taken without Indian consent.[33]

As a consequence of the Termination and Relocation policy, more than 60 percent of American Indians now live in urban areas,[34] refuting the persistent stereotype of the "authentic" rural Indian. According to the census of 2000, Los Angeles County has an Indian population of 76,988, in the category of one race/full blood; and 138,696, in the category of race alone or in combination with other races.[35] Los Angeles is recognized as having the largest concentration of American Indians in the United States.[36] A frequently asked question is, Where in Los Angeles do they live? There is no specific Indian neighborhood or ghetto; rather they are widely dispersed, as is true with Indians in other cities.[37]

The recognition that there was no particular geographic concentration of Indians in Los Angeles, that Indian people were dispersed throughout the city, was an essential factor in the founding of the Native American Ministry of the Presbyterian Church, one of the urban endeavors to which Viola has devoted significant time and energy.

The effort began in 1983 when an initial committee of five, including Viola Martinez, met to discuss strategies for meeting the needs of Indian people in Los Angeles. From this meeting emerged a long-range goal to develop a Native American Presbyterian ministry with two main objectives: (1) to provide a ministry for Indian people of Presbyterian faith who had not connected with a church since leaving the reservation, and (2) to raise the awareness of Presbyterian congregations regarding Native Americans as well as to include their cultural traditions in the work of the church by bringing Native American Presbyterians into leadership roles and developing new approaches of ministry.

The Special Committee on Native American Ministry of the synod of Southern California and Hawaii, as the committee came to be called, was created at the meeting of the synod in May 1983. From the original five-person working group, the committee grew to include other American Indians from the community as well as Presbyterians outside of Southern California. The project would be issue-centered, aimed toward effecting social change rather than providing social services.

From the beginning the Native American Ministry recognized that its work had to be directed and informed by Native Americans. There existed a sensitivity to the image of the church as an instrument for denying Indian religious beliefs and practices. The committee had no ambitions to Christianize the Los Angeles Indian community nor to entice them into joining the Presbyterian Church.

In 1985 the synod provided funding for the American Indian New Church Development Probe. The oversight body of the project was the Special Committee on Native American Ministry. The committee sought to identify American Indians within the boundaries of the synod of Southern California and Hawaii who had been or were presently members of the Presbyterian Church but were without an affiliation to a local church. The survey was also intended to determine if these Presbyterians would be willing to work together to form a new American Indian church development.

Among the findings was that Southern California, with the largest urban population of American Indians in the United States, had no Presbyterian church serving the Indian community. In fact, there was no Presbyterian church formed by and for American Indians anywhere in the southern or western regions of the country. The committee concluded that American Indian new church development might be extremely difficult yet exceptionally significant.

The Native American Ministry has provided Indians in the Los Angeles area with opportunities to worship and to build a sense of community. The founding of the ministry and its many benefits, as related in chapter 7, are achievements of which Viola is appropriately proud.[38]

The remaining chapters in this book together with those discussed here bring to fruition months of work and companionship in our endeavor to tell the remarkable life story of Viola Meroney Martinez.

1

Facing the Sunrise
Owens Valley

FOLLOWING THE DEATH OF HER MOTHER, IVY LENT Meroney, in the flu epidemic of 1918, Viola was raised by her maternal aunt, Mary Ann Brazzanovich. Vi was probably ten years old[1] when she was sent in 1927 from her home in Benton, California, in the Owens Valley to the Sherman Institute Federal Indian Boarding School in Riverside, California. Accustomed to living in a traditional Paiute home, which faces east, she had been transported to a school dormitory that evidently faced west. Viola recalls, "The thing that I remember, the first morning I woke up, the sun came up the wrong way. From the wrong direction. Where we lived in Benton the White Mountains were over here [to the east] and the sun always came up from this direction. I wondered what kind of world I had come into because the sun came up the wrong way, not in my face, but behind me. That I remember. And it took me a long time to adjust to that."[2]

To reach the locale where the sun came up the right way for Viola, one would drive on U.S. Highway 395 into northern Inyo County in east-central

California. The highway, one of California's most dramatic scenic routes, climbs from the Mojave Desert into Owens Valley, a sliver of green between two opposing mountain ranges with 14,000-foot peaks, the Sierra Nevada to the west and White-Inyo to the east. The Owens Valley Paiutes are the southernmost group of Northern Paiutes occupying northern Nevada and eastern California. Viola is a member of the Paiute group who were called by the Yokuts, their western neighbors, üt*ü' üt*ü witü, "the hot-place-people", because of the natural hot springs at Benton.[3]

Owens Valley Paiutes once controlled the narrow green region that encompasses both the headwaters and the terminus of the Owens River. Because of favorable ecological conditions, precontact Owens Valley people attained a degree of stability and sophistication unmatched elsewhere in the Great Basin.[4] An isolated but remarkable environment with artesian springs, high water tables, and fertile soil was enhanced by an irrigation system designed by the indigenous inhabitants.[5]

Recent estimates of the precontact population indicate two thousand Paiutes living in permanent villages throughout the valley.[6] The current population of enrolled Owens Valley Paiutes is also approximately two thousand, an estimated fifteen hundred of whom are living in the valley.[7] The people of Owens Valley once spoke dialects of Mono, a western Numic branch of the Uto-Aztecan language family.[8] Today, fluent speakers of the native language are virtually nonexistent.[9]

Which white explorers were the first to enter Owens Valley remains a mystery, although scholars generally agree that the argument for an expedition in the 1820s led by Jedediah Smith is plausible.[10] Existing documentation attests to explorations of Owens Valley beginning in the 1830s by fur trappers, the mountain men of western lore, notably Peter Skene Ogden and Joseph Reddeford Walker. John C. Frémont is believed to have explored Owens Valley in 1845, naming the valley, river, and lake in honor of his lieutenant, Richard Owens. Although historians

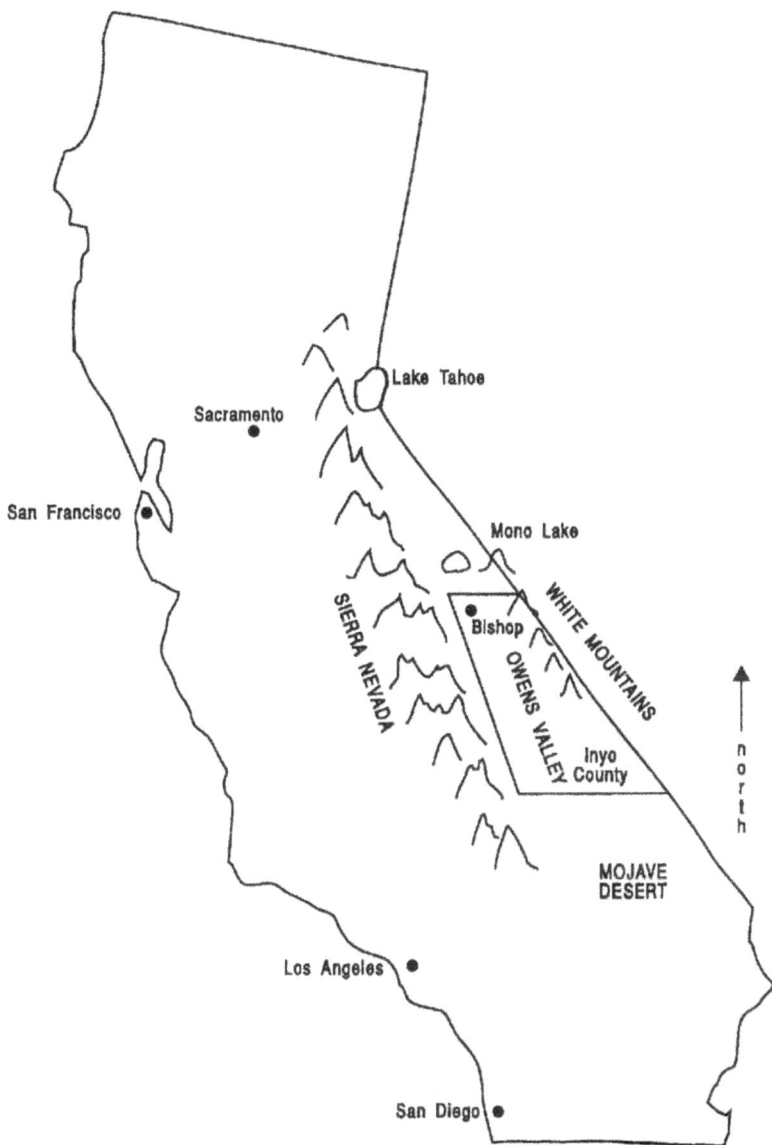

Map of California, with Owens Valley area indicated.

The Benton ranch. The owner of this ranch allowed Viola's uncle Bob Somerville and his family to live here for one dollar per year.
Photo by Burton Frasher (ca. 1900). Courtesy of Eastern California Museum.

differ on this point, Owens may not have participated in this trip and may never have seen the valley named for him.[11] Moreover, Harlan D. Unrau, historian for the National Park Service, asserts, "The namesake was Richard Owens, who *like Frémont*, had never seen the valley."[12]

Following the mountain men were the miners. Prospecting and mining began in the eastern Sierra in the early 1850s when a series of gold and silver strikes in the eastern Sierra area drew fortune seekers overflowing from the California Gold Rush of 1849. Mono County was first populated by this backwash of the Gold Rush wave. Mining in Owens Valley began in the late 1850s, with virtually all of the first mining camps situated on the east bank of the Owens River.[13] Benton, which for centuries had attracted Paiutes to its hot springs, became the supply center for the nearby mining districts. A pony express station was established at the Benton trading post.[14] Although activity in the area was slower than in other areas of eastern California, mining continued on a small scale for nearly half a century and eventually became woven in numerous ways into the Paiutes' lives.

Viola relates this story about her family's involvement in prospecting. These events took place as Vi and Mary Ann stopped at a ranch along their travels:

> This uncle came out to meet us and apparently this had been prearranged. . . . I'm sure that time was of the essence because it seemed to me, in no time at all, I was back in the buggy. . . . We went on out a ways from the ranch area to a creek. . . . I remember this big rock there. . . . They left me there and said, "You stay here. . . . Everything will be all right." Apparently I must have asked them, "How long?" That's when he said in Indian: "See that rock over there? When you see the shadow of the rock . . . and it comes to this point." He made a line. "We'll be back." . . . Sure enough, I was there when they came back. Sure enough there was that point just like he said. . . . They [had] picked up these small frying pans and a bucket and picks. . . . My aunt took this little bag that she had. . . . I think it was the next day, she brought out this little sack at my cousin [Mary Ann's son] Nick's place. She had these vials. Glass vials, little vials. I would say maybe one-half inch, three-quarter inch in diameter. They were full of this gold dirt . . . fine gold sand. I had no idea at the time what they were. They knew where to go. They knew exactly where to go. And they never, ever told anyone. . . . Now my cousin Nick had to know where [the gold] was, but he never, ever apparently told anybody. Isn't that something?[15]

The influx of miners created a market for products and services, so that with the decline in gold and silver mining, cattle ranching and farming brought settlers into the Owens Valley. Within one decade, the vast numbers of miners, followed by thousands of permanent settlers, completely disrupted the Native peoples' social and economic stability.[16]

Land claims had been filed by whites under the Homestead Act of 1862 and the Preemption Act of 1864, both of which required the claimants to live on and improve their land. The Paiutes' attractive irrigated fields were the first to be homesteaded.[17] Displaced from their homelands, the Paiutes were forced to adapt to labor on white-owned ranches. Viola provides an account of this traumatic impact:

> My uncle Bob Somerville said this [land in Benton] is where we always lived. This [rancher] Davis came in there, decided he wanted it, took it over, and started to farm it. . . . [Davis] let [my relatives] work for him. My uncle said, "We didn't have any place to go but they let us work for him. . . . My brother George [Washington] went to [Davis] and said that he wanted all of us to be able to live together and what could we do about it?" They worked it out and paid a dollar a year. I said, "Uncle Bob, you paid a dollar a year to live there?" He told me: "Yes, lots of money. A dollar a year, lots of money."
>
> To think that here is this fertile valley with a natural hot springs for the use of the people who had been living there for centuries, using it certain times of the year when they were able to grow the crops they were going to prepare for winter usage. . . . Then to come back to find it occupied by foreigners and told it was no longer theirs. Eventually working it out with [Davis] so they could live there for a dollar a year, when originally it was theirs. He should be paying them for the privilege that he had taken. To me, that's ironic.

Another irony in this displacement is that the indigenous people of Owens Valley had practiced agriculture on a wide scale in precontact times. In their valley, extending seventy-five miles from north to south and roughly six to ten miles from west to east, the Paiutes are believed to have constructed an elaborate irrigation system around A.D. 1000.[18]

In seeking to improve their food supply, Native Californians were sensitive to the critical need for maintaining balance in

Hot springs at Benton.
Photo by Burton Frasher. Courtesy of Eastern California Museum.

delicate ecosystems.[19] Although Owens Valley—in the rainless shadow of the Sierra Nevada—has a desert climate, heavy precipitation condensed from cloud masses travels down into the valley through rivulets and streams.[20] Swampy areas on the valley floor, as well as abundant water in Owens Lake and Mono Lake when full to capacity, made the Owens Valley very attractive to the thirsty metropolis of Los Angeles in the early 1900s. Although the valley is 233 miles from Los Angeles, the high-quality water now flows by gravity all the way to the city. The 338-mile-long Los Angeles Aqueduct has delivered since its completion in 1913 an average of 65 percent of the city's total water supply, 550 million gallons of water per day.[21]

In what the *Los Angeles Times* calls the "infamous appropriation of the Owens River and its tributaries,"[22] Los Angeles had bought by 1933 virtually all the land in Owens Valley. There had been a tense coexistence between Owens Valley and Los Angeles

Paiute village at Benton where Vi lived with Aunt Mary Ann. Photo by Burton Frasher (ca. 1900). Courtesy of Eastern California Museum.

between 1913 and 1919, when the city began buying more land in Owens Valley to acquire additional water rights.[23] A few cattle ranchers and sheep ranchers were given grazing leases without water rights, farmers were forced out of the valley, and the towns shriveled to arid ghosts.

After years of litigation, the city of Los Angeles in 1994 relinquished some of its Owens Valley water to save Mono Lake, in 1997 agreed to limit groundwater pumping, and in 1998 accepted responsibility for controlling toxic dust blowing from the dry bed of Owens Lake.[24]

The inhabitants of the valley who suffered the greatest

displacement were the eight hundred remaining Paiutes. Paiute land and water rights were protected by the federal government, but the lands allocated to them were too poor for cultivation. Their dependence on employment with white-owned ranches and farms proved disastrous as white settlers fled the area and farm labor virtually disappeared. The purchase of Owens Valley by Los Angeles had reduced by more than one-half the sources of Indian income.

In 1932 an official of the Los Angeles Department of Water and Power, appearing before a United States Senate Committee investigating Indian conditions throughout the country, testified that the Indians were destitute and suggested that they be relocated out of Owens Valley. He expressed concern that their deplorable living conditions, "in shacks, tents, wickiups, and hovels," were threatening contamination of not only the local water supply but also that of the city of Los Angeles.[25]

After years of irresolution concerning "the Indian problem," the city finally recognized its obligation to the Indians and negotiated a settlement, providing the Paiutes with better lands and assured water rights.[26] This agreement, the Land Exchange Act of 1937, created Paiute reservations at Bishop, Big Pine, and Lone Pine through a land trade between the U.S. Department of the Interior and the city of Los Angeles.[27] The Bishop Paiute Indian reservation comprised 875 acres; Big Pine, 279 acres; and Lone Pine, 237 acres. All three reservations function under the Trust Agreement of 1 April 1939 and the Assignment Ordinance of April 1962. The Assignment Ordinance was created to regulate the assignment of land on the reservations to enrolled tribal members.

Reservations had not been established in Owens Valley until after 1900. In 1902 a section of Fort Independence had been set aside for local Indians, but a reservation was not established at this location until 1915, the same year in which a small reserve was established at Benton. Following the enactment of the Land Exchange Act, the federal government constructed new housing and sewer and irrigation systems on the Bishop, Big Pine, and Lone Pine reservations. Fort Independence and Benton were not included in these improvements.

Remnants of the forced adaptation to wage labor on farms and ranches are found in the family names bestowed on Indian people by their white employers.[28] In identifying her aunt Mary Ann's brothers, Viola says: "The first ones I met that I realized were brothers to my aunt were George Washington, who was given that name by the rancher he worked for because he resembled George Washington, and Frank Couch, Uncle

George's brother. He, too, acquired his name in the same manner because the Indian names were hard to pronounce. It was easier to do this. When they once established themselves as part of a ranch group, why that was what took place."[29]

With the decline in mining and agriculture, scenic and recreational resources of the eastern Sierra became the foundation by the mid-1930s of the Owens Valley economy. With the completion in the late 1930s of Highway 395, which runs between the Mojave Desert and Lake Tahoe, Owens Valley became a year-round vacation destination.

In one of the most remarkable vignettes in her narration, Vi describes the calamitous impact tourism had on her family:

> There is a story. After Tom [in birth order] was Alice. . . . Oh, she was an adorable girl, they said. My mother worked in a laundry in town. Whenever Alice was around, the white people just loved her. One couple, particularly, took a real shine to her. When they would go up to the Mammoth Lake area, June Lake and all those places, they'd ask my mother if they could take [Alice] with them. The result was that they stole her.
>
> I really want to tell this story. To this day we don't know where she is. . . . Because it happened before I was born, I don't know anything about it directly. . . . My aunt [Mary Ann] told me there was another sister and she was stolen. This couple just took her up to the High Sierras and just never came back. Of course, anything that happened to the Indians, the whites didn't care. . . . Nobody did anything about it.
>
> [Vi's sister] Edith tried for a long time to find [Alice]. She came to Los Angeles and she went to different agencies to see if there was some way they could trace her, and there was just no way they could. . . . [Also] they didn't have any money. Nobody had the money to pursue anything like that.
>
> I wonder if this book would bring her out? Wouldn't that be something?[30]

Viola's uncles (all brothers, despite different last names): Joe Lent, Jack Lent, Dick Reuben, and Billy Williams. Although it is certain that this photo depicts all four brothers, neither Vianne Wentzell, Viola's daughter, nor I can positively identify the names of the brothers according to their positions in the photo. Vianne says: "My mom felt the care and concern all her uncles had for her welfare. With Paiutes everyone is a sister, brother, cousin, aunt, or uncle." Courtesy of Viola Martinez.

2

"A Mess of Uncles"
Viola's Early Years

VIOLA WAS SENT TO SHERMAN INSTITUTE BY HER
extended family—a "mess of uncles" who had
decided that the federal Indian boarding school
was the most advantageous place for her to be.
"The funny part about all these uncles," she says,
"is they had different last names."[1] All of them,
however, were vitally interested in her welfare.

The Paiute kinship ethic requires that one take
care of one's relatives, especially old people and
children. Concern for children is manifested when
relatives take in the children of parents who have
died or divorced, claiming that these children
"belong to the family."[2] Vi articulated this ethic
when I became frustrated in attempting to con-
struct her family tree. The tangle of relationships
was complicated. Siblings may have different sur-
names, some because their names were imposed by
white employers, others because siblings had
different fathers. Viola's advice: "Constructing a
family tree is not the important thing. We are all
family. We help each other like family. That's what's

important."[3] Viola and I have, however, identified individuals as distinctly as possible within the context of her story.

In reviewing documents in Viola's file from the National Archives,[4] what emerged dramatically was a discernible variance between statements in the files and her life history as she recalls it. She explains the discrepancy: "Indians kept no written records, and non-Indians couldn't care less whether they recorded accurate information about Indians."[5] This cavalier attitude on the part of white record-keepers was especially problematic to Vi because during her twelve years at boarding school she was isolated from her Paiute community and thus disconnected from oral tradition, which would have fixed her more securely in time and place. In reviewing documents relating to her being sent to Sherman Institute, Viola was distraught over statements that she was an orphan with no home. "I never considered myself an orphan. That's white man's terminology. If my aunt were alive she would throw a fit. I had a lovely home with her. She took real good care of me. I was the cleanest little girl on the reservation."[6]

Not knowing her birth date has been a lifelong frustration for Viola. She has been told that she was born in a hospital in Bishop, but the records were destroyed in a fire. Since she knows her mother died in the 1918 flu epidemic, Viola, the youngest of her mother's children, most likely was born in 1917. Viola tries to sort out the relationships:

> I was told by my aunt that my mother had ten children. The only brothers that I know of are Hiram and Tom. Hiram, from what I understand, was the fourth birth child she had, because [before Hiram] she had Edith, Edna, and Leora. I'm not sure but there must have been a birth in between there someplace, because I'm sure from having seen my brother Tom, and having seen my other brother, Hiram, only once, it seemed to me they were much older. They were not close enough [to the other siblings] in birth. I don't know of any name I can insert in there. Then Alice comes into the

Viola's aunt Mary Ann Brazzanovich.
Photographer and date unknown. Courtesy of Viola Martinez.

picture, and Winona and myself. There's Edith, Edna, Leora, Hiram, Tom, space, Alice, space, Winona, me."[7]

Every time I would ask about my father, all I learned is that there are four of us that are Meroneys. There's Hiram, Tom, Winona, and myself, and of course, it would have been Alice, too, I suppose. [Later] I asked Winona about this, and she didn't know anything either. She said, "We were away, Vi. Those things weren't important to us. Now that they are important, there is nobody to tell us."

I know that there was a Sullivan Meroney, and there was a grandmother, Dolly Meroney. Dolly Meroney was *Hutsi*. *Hutsi* is the grandmother on the father's side. Sullivan Meroney was her son. Now whether Sullivan Meroney was our parent or not, I don't know. Winona doesn't know that either.[8]

Aunt Mary Ann would talk about Hutsi. . . . She was definitely Paiute. Winona said she tried to ask Leora about it. Leora said, "That's old stuff. You don't want to hear anything about that." They just didn't want to talk about it for some reason.

Viola knows very little about her father, other than that he was half Paiute. About her mother she recounts the following:

My aunt wouldn't talk about her. My uncles wouldn't talk about her. I remember asking [one uncle] what kind of person she was. All he said was that she was a beautiful woman. . . . [Aunt Mary Ann and my mother] were half-sisters. Now that is an interesting story. This Indian, apparently was a real—maybe "macho male" is what you would call him. That's just my idea from the little things my aunt said. He married two sisters. Yes, Indian way. He had two wives.[9]

The reason this came up is because I was meeting so many uncles and aunts, and I was beginning to realize the white man's way of determining who was really related. With Indians, you're [all] cousins. You know you are related the Indian way. After my mother died and I came to live with my aunt, I was meeting uncles . . . my uncle so-and-so, my uncle this, my uncle that. Finally I asked my aunt how come I had so many uncles. My uncle Joe had a different last name. Uncle Bill, Billy Williams, had a different name. George Washington had a different name. . . . Anyway, there are a mess of uncles. So, I asked, "How come?" [Aunt Mary Ann] said, "Two sisters." My mother's and my aunt's parents. Their father had two [wives].[10]

A significant uncle in Vi's life was Joe Lent. "He spoke super English. He could read and write. It seemed to me he was great. He taught us, my uncle's children and myself, Christmas carols. . . . I asked my aunt again, "Whose brother is he?" She would say, "It doesn't make any difference. What's the matter with you?"

Bob Somerville, Viola's uncle.
Courtesy of Viola Martinez.

Viola persisted because her mother was a Lent, Ivy Lent. "That's how I learned that Joe Lent was my mother's brother."

Viola barely remembers that she and her sister Winona lived briefly with Jack Lent, Joe's brother, after their mother died and before Vi went to live with Aunt Mary Ann and Winona went to boarding school in Stewart, Nevada. "There is very little I remember . . . but I remember they made a big fire. It was in the evening. . . . We used to sit in the old wagons and we'd turn the wheels, you know. [Winona] and I were turning the wheels, and I got my finger caught in it. I remember that it was Uncle Jack that got after us." She is sure they were not just visiting, but actually living with the Lent family. "We went to bed there and everything. We didn't go away. We were there."[11]

Eventually, after completing her schooling, Vi returned to Owens Valley and became acquainted with all the Lents, but she echoes her aunt's sentiments: "We were one family; all of those people were there, helping, making sure we were taken care of. That's the reason I mention them the way I do, because they are my family."

She especially remembers the Somerville uncles:

My aunt was visited particularly by John Somerville. He was an uncle. One of her kin. He had a brother, Bob Somerville. . . . Joe Lent and Uncle Bob, I think, were very well liked by the white people. I guess [the uncles] were not resentful. In fact, my aunt used to say they were telling [the white people] too many things. She didn't like the way [the whites] could ask them anything. They would always get an answer and it was always the right answer. The others, sometimes, wouldn't give the whites the true facts. . . . Uncle Joe and Uncle Bob were well-spoken, and they were well thought of. Uncle Bob did well as a prospector. I have a feeling my aunt was helped by him occasionally, because we never lacked for money when we really needed it.[12]

A name that occurs frequently throughout Vi's narrative is that of her husband's uncle, Tom Gustie, whom she met when he visited Sherman Institute. Although he was visiting children directly related to his wife, he made a point of also contacting Viola. "Because he felt sorry for me. He apparently knew of me when I was little at home. . . . He must have known my relatives in Benton. They were all over the place. He might even have been related to them way back. . . . Really, if it hadn't been for him, I never would have gotten away [from the boarding school] at all. No one else ever visited me."[13]

Viola's affection for Tom Gustie is echoed in the feelings of her daughter Vianne: "Grandpa Tom. He was really Uncle Tom, but I always called him Grandpa Tom. . . . I felt really comfortable in his house. . . . He was very easy to be with. He was kind."[14]

Sheila Gustie Martinez[15] remembers her father:

My dad, he was a hard worker. From what I understand, he had a fourth-grade education. He dropped out of school when he knew how to read. He was self-educated after that. He was a man who took care of his family. Everyone thought he owned millions. . . because he was able to save. He never spent money for himself.

He'd plant hay in the back acres and make extra money by selling the bales. He got some cattle. He started out with two. That grew into maybe about fifteen. He'd keep them long enough to sell them for beef, just for extra money. When he needed a car, he would go down and pay cash. That's why they thought we were really rich. . . . His main work was as a carpenter. I guess in the beginning he came down to L.A. quite a bit. He worked for a lot of contractors in Los Angeles. After his mother got sick, he had to move back [to Owens Valley], I guess, because of the land. By then Mammoth [California] and all that area was developing.

Then he was also involved in the tribal stuff around there. He was interested in the community, not only advancing his family. Overall, he was interested, deep down, in the community.[16]

No one is remembered by Viola more vividly or more appreciatively than Aunt Mary Ann. Vi describes going when she was four or five years old with her aunt down to the hot springs in Benton to get water:

> There were lard cans with handles. They were thick cans with little handles on them. She would take a couple of big buckets and she would have me go down there [with her]. She would do a number of things [at the hot springs.] She would wash clothes. She would wash my hair. I would go in the little sort of pond that was filled in. [Afterward] the water would be released and let run down into the meadows. . . . There was a big tank out in front of Aunt Mabel's house and Uncle George's house. Mabel is his daughter, but I call her Aunt Mabel. The tank was where everyone could get to it. . . . Anyone who went down there [to the hot springs] would always make sure they came back with water to put in the tank to get it cold so we could use it."[17]

As a young child, traveling with Aunt Mary Ann on her trade route made a profound impact on Viola.

> [Aunt Mary Ann] was very independent. She always was ready to do things for herself. If there was a place she wanted to go or things she wanted to do, she would just go and do it. The rest of my relatives held back and acted more the Indian way [shy]. . . . She insisted she had to have a horse and buggy. . . . She took good care of that horse in Benton because that was her means of getting away. . . . When she would leave, naturally, she would take me. I barely remember going from Benton over Mono Pass or up through Mono Lake and going up Tioga Pass, up to the top, and going down the other side to Yosemite [National Park] in her buggy. My aunt had to walk because the buggy carried the hay and oats and our belongings.[18]

Aunt Mary Ann evidently was extremely well-organized, packing the buggy so as to be able to use things in the order needed and not packing anything not needed. When things were used along the way, they were replaced by items she could use later at home. The last thing packed was a bale of hay upon

Paiute women washing clothes in the Benton hot springs.
Photo by Burton Frasher. Courtesy of Eastern California Museum.

which Vi sat as long as the road was level. When they came to an incline, Vi got out of the wagon and walked up the hill, while her aunt walked the horse around the curves.

She would boil eggs and she would pack them. Her intent, usually, was not to go for a week or so but two or three months in the summer and come back in the fall. I recall that when we went into the High Sierra before you get to Mono Lake, she would start looking for people. Of course, at first I didn't know who she was looking for. Then we would see the dust. She would, in Indian, say, "*Eeo, eeo, eeo.*" That means "Over there, over there." ... It seemed to me they had a meeting place, because she would go to a certain spot and stop. I knew she planned to spend the night there because she would put the horse out to wander around. She would start making her little camp. In the evening, I remember, these two men came, and they spoke a different kind of broken English, not in the way Indians spoke a

Benton trading post, the supply center for the nearby mines in the 1850s. Photo by Burton Frasher (circa 1900). Courtesy of Eastern California Museum.

broken English. They were white. They were sheepherders. They would be carrying things with them. . . . They seemed to know her. This was probably a yearly, summer thing for her to go up and see her family and trade with the sheep-herders. I remember this: she gave them the eggs. They were delighted, really delighted in the eggs. That's what they were for, for them. She ended up with sheepherder bread, legs of lamb. She ended up with wine, this red wine. Oh, and she always gave them her basketry.[19]

American sheep ranchers had imported Basque sheep-herders from the Pyrenees into the American West in the mid-1800s. One of California's main sheep trails ran up the spine of the Eastern Sierra. The annual spring journey with the sheep began in Bakersfield, California, then traversed Walker Pass into the Mojave Desert, moving north through Owens Valley and finally summering in the mountain meadows of the Sierra Nevada. Aunt Mary Ann was perhaps the only woman among

Heavy steel doors designed to protect the silver deposited by miners at Benton trading post, a Wells Fargo Express silver depot.
Photo by Burton Frasher. Courtesy of Eastern California Museum.

Sheep at Benton ranch. Viola's aunt Mary Ann traded
with the Basque sheepherders who traversed the trail
that ran up the spine of the Eastern Sierra.
Photo by Burton Frasher. Courtesy of Eastern California Museum.

those people who replenished the sheepherders' supplies and
provided their only contact with the outside world.[20]

One of the stops on Aunt Mary Ann's route was Yosemite
National Park. When the National Park Service was created in
1916, Yosemite officials and merchants introduced "Indian field
days," ostensibly intended to reinvigorate Indian arts, presumably including the fine Paiute basketry. The field days quickly
degenerated into stereotypical presentations of Plains Indians.[21]
Vi recalls her experience with Indian field days:

> Yearly they had a big Indian festival where the people in
> charge of [Yosemite] Park paid the Indians to come.... They
> would camp in there, and they would have this big cere-
> mony. The first time I saw it, there was a live play where there
> were horses and houses were burning, Indians coming
> around and setting fire to them. I thought the Indians were
> terrible.... I was little.... I didn't even know what it was all
> about. All I knew was that the Indians were horrible. They
> were coming in and killing the whites.[22]

Collection of Paiute baskets of Mrs. D. V. Cain of Bodie, California.
Some of the baskets are believed to have been woven by Viola's
aunt Mary Ann.
Photo by Burton Frasher. Courtesy of Eastern California Museum.

Vi remembers that there were two places to which Aunt
Mary Ann made a point of going.

This was what people just knew she would do. One was to
go up to Bridgeport [California] to visit her son [Nick] and
the other was to go to Bishop to visit all the other relatives.
. . . We'd go up to the Mono mills area where we went down
the other side. . . . Coming on down into Mono Lake and up
around and over Conway Summit to Bridgeport. . . . Apparently she had been doing it quite some time, because she
seemed to know everyone and they knew her. They sort of
expected her. It was a natural thing for her to do the laundry
for them and do the ironing and even help in the cooking.
She would be paid in food or money, or even in material
[fabric]. I remember one time, it probably was at Mono
mills, she did get some pretty material. . . .

Then, of course, the next place we stopped was at Mono Lake, and she worked for the family that ran the store there. Then over on the other side, between the lake and the pass, Conway Summit, was the Mono Inn Lodge, owned by the McPhersons. Wherever she went the people hired her. She probably said to them: "I need money. I need work." She always seemed to work and she always ended up with money.[23]

Viola remembers having her first taste of tapioca pudding at the McPhersons. On one of their stops there they were served lunch with the other workers by Mrs. McPherson. Vi was very reluctant to try the pudding. "It looked pretty strange with all those little lumps." She was persuaded to taste it, being assured that she would like it. "And I really did!"[24]

Another first for Vi was cake batter. She and her aunt, traveling near what is now the town of Lee Vining, visited a relative, Minnie Turner. The Turners worked for a rancher and lived in a cabin. Vi watched as Minnie mixed cake batter and was curious what it was. Minnie let her own kids taste the uncooked batter and Vi was intrigued that they obviously enjoyed it so much; but she did not ask for a taste, and apparently Minnie did not think to offer her one. Later, she did have some of the baked cake, but she promised herself that when she was grown she would make cakes and let her kids taste the batter. Doing so for Vianne and Kirk is one of her fondest memories, especially because she told them the story of her introduction to cake.[25]

Aunt Mary Ann's husband had died before Viola had a chance to meet him. His last name was Brazzanovich, but Vi does not know what his first name was. Vi is aware that when her aunt was widowed, "She tried to do for herself as much as possible. If she wasn't able to, her brothers and others would help. We always had food. They always made sure we had sacks of flour and sacks of potatoes and things of that sort."[26]

After traveling all summer with Aunt Mary Ann, Viola sometimes would be late starting school in Benton in the fall because she would first go pine-nutting with her aunt and other relatives. Piñons, the typical pines of eastern California, are scrubby trees that produce tons of protein-rich pine nuts annually. Although Viola's memories of the harvests float up vividly in her narration, she cautions, "My memory may not be completely clear. Others may remember more accurately."[27]

They start harvesting the nuts [in] the later part of August, into September and October. There are two stages that are important. One is where we prepare the pine nuts for use, not only for the winter months, but also into the [following] summer. To do that we cook the pine nuts in the cone. Out in the fields where the piñon trees are. We end up with big camps in areas depending on how the trees have grown and the pine nuts have ripened. . . . We shake the trees and use sticks to knock the branches so that the cones will drop down. We get [both] solid cones, which won't pop open, and cones that are already open. With these [open cones] the youngsters start gathering the pine nuts [that have fallen to the ground].

They have big canvases under the trees so that when the cones drop, the men—this is where the men work with the women—they go in and start gathering the cones with the nuts in them. They start loading them into our utility baskets. . . . Now, when you cook the pine nuts in the cone and you shell them later, they come out like peanuts. They are crisp.

When you cook the pine nuts outside of the cone, they come out soft. Then you have to let those dry. The pine nuts cooked in the cone are for ongoing use. You can store them. Where, if you cook the pine nuts outside the cone, they have to be used within a certain time.

Now when we cook these loose nuts, we have winnowing baskets. . . . They are wide, like a pan, but they are willow. Minnie [Williams], Eleanor's mother and my mother's cousin, knew just exactly when to get the embers out of the fire, because she didn't want them to turn to ashes, but she wanted them to cook the nuts. She got the nuts ready, pine nuts in the shell all in a little bundle. Then she put a few embers in and started to work the basket. Of course the basket had a little scorch, but it didn't burn. She had a way of shaking it. Imagine the taste of those nuts!

The men have cleared a big area. In the middle of that they set up the bonfire where they are going to cook the pinecones. I'm trying to remember. I have to think back. It seems to me that at the bottom they had boulders. Good-sized stones. The sage that is green and still growing is put on top of the boulders. Then the brown sage that will burn is next. . . .

And it's left that way. Around the sides you will see piles of sage. Then they bring in the embers from the burned sage. They put that in as they are going along. As they are piling up the cones, they have embers underneath.

Then they pile up more and more cones on this platform that they made with the stones and sage. At first I thought it was funny the way they placed the cones. Why do they have to be so particular? Why don't they just dump the cones on there. But they don't. The have a way of placing them because they need ventilation.

They make a fire on top of the cones. I remember asking, "Isn't it going to burn up the pine nuts?" They said no, because they know when to stop building the fire. When it's time, they start raking off some of the embers. Then they pile dirt on top of the whole thing. That's the beauty of it. It makes an oven. It steams [the cones]. This is just they way they do it.

Meanwhile the young ones are out there picking under the trees filling our baskets. They had games going for us kids, they enticed us, encouraging us to go out and work hard, so that we were all of us working and enjoying it. Then, of course, while all of this is going on, the women are preparing other spots for cooking the cones.

It seems to me the first time I went, we left Benton early. When we got there fires were going and people were eating breakfast. Some were working on these mounds. I wondered what those mounds were. I found out, naturally, what they were. People came from Nevada, I recall. Some came over from Yosemite.

This would go on for a couple of months. The pine-nutting season is from the time that they start to ripen until they are all ripened. That's up into October. We would camp out the whole time, and it was a time when they visited. And they had games. They had horse races. They had card games, too. There was [a game called] Ten Cards, *Chepatooie*. There were always things for the youngsters to do. It was a fun time. [28]

Paiute woman, identified as Mary Lent, winnowing pine nuts.
Photo by A. A. Forbes. Courtesy of Eastern California Museum.

Minnie Williams winnowing pine nuts, late 1970s. Minnie is Viola's cousin-in-law.
Courtesy of Eleanor Bethel.

Vi's daughter, Vianne, remembers going when she was a child into the mountains in the fall to harvest pine nuts, as does Vi's son, Kirk. Kirk remembers, "I didn't do the pine-nutting myself. I just did the running around. But I watched the elders gather the nuts and put them on the fire and into the baskets."[29]

Vi's niece Sheila, Tom Gustie's daughter, remembers going annually with her brothers: "They'd make a big family thing out of it. We'd make sure we'd be up there to join in. . . . My older brother will [still] take the kids. But, of course, the kids are older now and they have other interests."[30] Viola believes the last time she went pine-nutting was in the late 1980s. She doubts if anyone is harvesting pine nuts anymore. "All the oldsters are gone. . . . Time is so important in today's world that you can't take time out to go and live the way you would like to."[31]

Vi's memories of her early years in Owens Valley were enhanced by our visit with Harry and Grace Keller.[32] Harry is Vi's second-cousin, the son of her cousin Mabel, who was the daughter of her mother's brother. Both Harry and Vi remembered Vi's starting school late in the fall because of pine-nutting. "You caught up with the rest of us in a month. . . . They even let you get ahead of us," Vi recalls Harry saying, "grumpy like." She remembers that she did skip a grade. Because of her performance in the school in Benton, her uncles decided to send her to boarding school. "Joe Lent really felt that we needed to learn the white man's way." Aunt Mary Ann, however, complained, "Why are you taking her now when she can be of help to me and we can do things together?" The response was that Vi was growing up, could not attend the school in Benton much longer, and the school in Bishop would not accept Indians.[33]

Current research reveals a growing number of accounts by Indian boarding school graduates that express ambivalence about the boarding school experience.[34] Viola felt ambivalent from the moment she learned from her aunt that she was being sent away to school. "I didn't want to go because I just didn't know what I was getting into." However, she also remembers

Schoolhouse in Benton that Viola attended.
Photographer unknown. Courtesy of Viola Martinez.

her much older sister Leora coming back to Owens Valley from boarding school. "She was dressed real nice. She appeared happy. What little I remember, she sounded like [boarding school] was nice."[35]

Aunt Mary Ann, however, was not ambivalent. Vi recalls, "She was upset. She was really upset." Documents in the National Archives indicate that her uncle, John Somerville, acting as Vi's guardian, signed the necessary papers, but Viola distrusts the signature. "It's too fine. Too well written for a person for whom English is difficult. The writing is beautiful." She has no explanation for this inconsistency.[36]

She recalls the first official word that she was being sent to a boarding school: "It must have been somebody from the government, because he came [to her aunt's home] in this car, and the only cars that they had in those days belonged to government people."[37] On the day of her departure she felt "lost" when she saw another car approaching early in the morning to pick her up. Her aunt was desolate. "She cried. Of course I did, too. She said we probably would never see each other again. . . . She figured maybe she would be dead by the time I returned."[38]

Viola remembers that five children made the trip from Owens Valley to Riverside in a car, driven by a man she assumes was Paiute, although she is not sure about this. The only thing she remembers clearly about arriving at Sherman Institute that evening were the tall palm trees, which she had never seen before. "It seemed everywhere you looked were these palm trees."[39]

The children with whom she had made the daylong trip were all taken to an austere building, a dormitory named Minnie Ha Ha. Viola was assigned to a sleeping porch that housed three other girls. She did not know these girls; they were not Paiute, but "they were Indians, so it wasn't bad." However, she notes the following: "Other than the fact that we, as youngsters, latched on to one another, it was a very cold environment. There was nothing to make you feel like you were in a family. I had never been in this kind of situation where there were no mountains, nothing, around. Here I am where there's only a few strange buildings and a different kind of trees. I truly felt that I was really far away from home."[40]

Detail from photo on page 59.

3

Far from Home
Sherman Institute
Boarding School

SHERMAN INSTITUTE FEDERAL INDIAN BOARDING School, sixty miles south of Los Angeles in a citrus-growing community, was a quarter of a century old when Viola Meroney Martinez was sent there in 1927. Built in 1902, it is the last constructed and the largest boarding school of the federal system.[1] While research on Sherman Institute is surprisingly meager, brief allusions to the school in the literature replicate the experiences of painful confusion and alienation that have been documented in studies of other Indian boarding schools, such as Carlisle Indian School, Pennsylvania; Haskell Institute, Lawrence, Kansas; Flandreau Indian Boarding School, South Dakota; and Chilocco Indian School, Oklahoma.[2]

Don Talayesva, a Hopi, recalled his years at Sherman Institute: "At that time I was half-Christian and half-heathen, and often wished there was some magic that could change my skin into that of a white man."[3] Another Hopi, Polingaysi Quoyawayma, described her experience at Sherman Institute succinctly: "Land of oranges, land of perfume. Time of torture."[4]

In her narration Viola never refers to Sherman Institute as harshly as do Talayesva and Polingaysi. Still, her experience was more negative than that of the majority of her peers, including her relatives, because, unlike her peers, she did not go home for twelve years.

Compared to Viola's home in Owens Valley, Sherman Institute was different in every way. When asked about her first night at Sherman Institute, Vi relates the following: "I was going to say it was real quiet. But, no, it wasn't always quiet. When we first got there I remember hearing this noise, and it was a streetcar. It made a little different sound than a car would make. Sort of a truck sound. You would hear a bell now and then. But when the streetcars weren't running, it was real, real quiet. You didn't hear birds. You didn't hear any animals."

Vivid in her memory is the smell surrounding the boarding school. "We were practically in the middle of a big orange grove and you could smell the flowers. They had a nice smell. [Later when] they were picking, they would come with truckloads of oranges and just dump them. We would all go out and get whatever containers we could to pick up oranges to eat because they just had too doggone many."[5]

Students complained in the 1931 yearbook *Smudgepot* of another environmental element caused by the proximity of the citrus groves. "Smudge! Smudge! Smudge! Smudge got into their noses, and on their clothes, and down their throats. When, at last, warmer days and nights came, they said goodbye to smudge for another year and welcomed sunshine."[6]

One of the most frequent and bitter recollections of former students concerns insufficient and inferior boarding school food.[7] This contrasts with Viola's memories: "We were very well fed. . . . We had a farm, a school farm. The boys ran that farm, provided the hogs, the chickens, the turkeys. There were orchards there." Her impression was that, rather than being meager, the meals were overabundant. "Often the kids just left food. It didn't bother them. I think that after a time I was that way too. But, initially, I do recall that I thought, 'Gosh, they waste so much food.'"[8]

Despite good nutrition, Viola remembers that among the children there was "a lot of illness. It seemed to me there were always real sick children in the hospital. . . . Tuberculosis was very common. I remember that. And before I went to Sherman, I used to hear [Indian people] say that a lot of the children from Sherman came back dead. They would say, 'Well, they will probably be shipped back dead.' In fact, the one time that I did go home, I escorted my cousin in a casket to the reservation."[9]

"When I was told she had TB," Vi recalls, "I felt very, very bad about it. . . .I always went to visit her. The hospital was right by the school, real close. I spent a lot of time with her. When she died they asked me to take her back. . . . We did it by train . . . the body, you know."[10]

Historian J. R. Miller points out that, despite such negative, even traumatic events, there are too many former boarding school students who view the experience on balance as positive "to justify ignoring or downplaying such memories."[11] Viola remembers some of the positive aspects: "[Sherman Institute] had inside bathroom facilities. They had electricity. They had running water. . . . I liked these changes. If you wanted to go get a drink, you didn't have go down to the spring or to the water tank, just to the drinking fountain. It was really good."[12]

Her admiration for the conveniences of electricity and running water was shaded by her anxiety about being ready for bed on time every night. "You had to have your teeth brushed and you had to be ready. When it was time for 'lights out' you had to be in bed. If you were not, you were punished by having to stand outside for an indefinite time."

Her anxiety was created by the absolute power of regimentation, which David Adams describes as "patently militaristic."[13] Viola hated "having to watch the clock":

Everything was done by the clock. I knew how to tell time, but I didn't realize that it governed you. It didn't govern us at home, but there [at Sherman Institute] it definitely did. I did not like the routine, because we were so regimented. Everything we did had to be done in a certain manner at a certain time and, in many cases, in a certain place. . . . There were days when you went to school in the morning and worked at chores in the afternoon. Then you would be changed. You would go to school in the afternoon and in the morning you would do all the necessary chores to keep this big institution running like a home, an everyday place of living. . . . You learned to cook. You washed, you ironed. You did the sewing and you did the cleaning. . . . For the fellows it was the same. The boys worked in the dining room because one thousand youngsters were served [meals] there. The boys did the heavy cooking in the kitchen, and the girls did the waiting on the tables and the preparing of some food. All those things while watching the clock."

Viola describes a typical day:

At 6:00 A.M. there was this triangle thing. It was good-sized and you could hear it throughout the dorms. The triangle got us up, then in forty-five minutes, it would go again. This meant "Out front, line up." From there you would go to the dining room, which was quite a way from the dorm. Of course, it is a community dining room. Breakfast at 7:00. You were given forty-five minutes to eat your breakfast. Line up again and go back to the dormitories. Get ready for school. At 9:00 you were ready to go to your first class. Those that were going to work would go to their work projects. Line up. Go to the group you were involved with. Then at 11:30 a regular siren would go off to let everybody know that it would be time to eat in a half hour. You would go back to your dorms and line up. At 12:00 line up, then go back to the dining room for lunch. Then at 12:30, line up and go back to the dorms. At 1:00 you went to your afternoon detail. Those that were in school in the morning would go to work, and those that were working in the morning would to the class rooms. Dismissal was usually around 4:00. You would line up and go back to your respective dorms. You had about an hour and a half free time before lining up for dinner. Of course after dinner you had your study hours. If you didn't have studies, you had to be quiet in your room. I read an awful lot. At 9:00 you had to be ready for bed.[14]

Viola remembers that Sundays had their own unique structure:

On Sundays, particularly, there was definite regimentation [because] people came to see the school. We performed every Sunday for people to come and watch us. If you were in Company A you had to be in Company A. You made sure you were always with your company. We had this long parade ground. The companies started out, and the march-ing band was way up at the other end. The band started down the field and the companies came around to the front. We had uniforms of white tops and navy pleated skirts that we wore only for marching. Every Sunday there were always big crowds there. They came from all over, I guess. There were huge, huge groups. [Sherman Institute was] showing off, I guess, supposedly doing something good for the Indians, [demonstrating that] we brought the children here, and we're educating them, teaching them how to act. Disci-pline. Your companies made sure they did their thing [prop-erly]. You had to perform just like you would, I guess, in the military service.[15]

As with all federal Indian boarding schools, the children at Sherman were required to go to church on Sundays, an essen-tial factor in their becoming "civilized."[16] Viola describes her early experiences with religion.

When I was very, very small, my uncle Joe Lent came to Benton, and he was involved—I don't know how much—

with missionaries. We went to the school building there to church, and after that we went to my other uncle's house. His name was George Washington. The wee little ones were singing "Silent Night," and we wanted to learn it. So he taught us to sing "Silent Night." And he talked about God.

Everybody went to church at the schoolhouse where there would be missionaries, and afterwards they would have a potluck. I remember there used to be food. It was probably a way for the Indians to get together. Every opportunity they had, they would get together. The thing that made an impression on me [about the church service] were the three hearts. One was black, one was white, and one was red. They were up at the front on the long blackboard they had there. The only thing I remember distinctly about them is that we didn't want to have black hearts. We apparently all had hearts, and it could be red, black, or white. You didn't want a black heart; you wanted a white heart. That's what we Indian children had to realize: we wanted to change our black hearts to white hearts, and that by believing in God, we could. Can you imagine, we started out with black hearts? We could get rid of them by becoming Christians. We were sinners. We were bad people, but we could learn to be good people. They did say, "Your Indian ways are bad. You have to learn white man's ways, and if you don't you are punished." I think at that tender age it didn't bother me, you know, the red, black, and white. In fact, it probably was interesting for the little ones. We probably thought, "Heck, we don't want to be black or red, so we are going to do everything to be white."[17]

The thing that I noticed when I went to Sherman was that there was a Protestant church and there was a Catholic church. . . . One of the first things we were asked, "What church are you going to go to?" I didn't realize there was more than one church. . . . I didn't know which one to go to. . . . I must have said something about the church where we went [in Benton]. I think I said the schoolhouse in Benton. On that basis they knew [which church I should attend]. I remember Miss White was the lady who took us to and from the church on Sundays. She was not the preacher, but she was his helper. She lived there on the campus, and any time Protestant children had problems, we would be sent to her for counseling. The Catholics would be sent to the father over at their church.

All of a sudden it bothered me. I remember that. Here's two churches, and we had to pick one of those. Why? And for the first time, I think, it did concern me. How come we can't go to one of our own? Why don't we have a church for Indians, just Indians? We had to choose one of the white churches. I never even had to think about it before. The only church there [in Benton] was the one in the school-house. . . . We weren't told that we had to go. It was just someplace for the community. . . . Now, all of a sudden, I go to Sherman, and the sun comes up in the wrong place, and then I'm told I have to pick a place to go to church. . . . Christianizing us was the whole idea. . . . One night a week we would be taken to the church, and they would have a Bible study. Midweek Sunday school. . . . I was trying to understand about Jesus dying on the cross. . . . I asked, "What's going to happen to my people?" I wanted to know . . . well, all I knew was that this man had died for white people. I guess my thought was "Who's dying for the Indians?"

I don't recall what response I got. [The person who was instructing us] probably said we were there being Christianized, we're there being civilized, we're being educated. We were told to forget our ways. I can't talk my language anymore. I can't talk and think about things in the past anymore because that's dumb. It's old stuff. You are coming into something entirely different. You are going to have to learn the way white people live. . . . Apparently [his response] was simple enough that I didn't question him anymore. I didn't have enough background of my own, really.[18]

As she grew older Viola realized that the Presbyterian Church was "pretty well in evidence throughout the High Sierra" and that the church the children at Sherman attended was probably determined by the missionary group to which they had been exposed. She considers herself a devout Christian, "very definitely a gradual development" which began at Sherman Institute. As an adult she reconciled her family's ethics with those of Christianity.[19]

In addition to Christianity, the other inextricable factor in "civilizing" Indian children was the prohibition of native languages, a brutal assault on the students' identity. Thomas Jefferson Morgan, commissioner of Indian affairs from 1889 to 1893, was the architect of the federal system for the education of Indian children.[20] With the support of humanitarian reformers, Morgan submitted his comprehensive plan to the secretary of the interior on 1 December 1889: "Education . . . is the Indians' only salvation. With it they will become honorable, useful, happy citizens of a great republic, sharing on equal terms in all its blessings. Without it they are doomed either to destruction or to hopeless degradation." Insistence upon the use only of English was a critical aspect of Morgan's plan: "Especial attention should be directed toward giving them a ready command of English. . . .[T]o this end, only English should be allowed to be spoken."[21]

Viola's narration provides an intimate depiction of her collision with the English-only decree:

I did want to speak my language, my Paiute language. And every chance I got I did. My cousins . . . well, most of them were my cousins, and I would sneak away and we would talk Paiute. I remember they had palm trees, tall palm trees there at Sherman. My cousin, Evelyn . . . we called her Fuzzy . . . and I would climb up where we wouldn't be seen or heard. . . . Because we were told: "If you hear anybody talking in their tribal language, you tell us." They told us we would be punished if we spoke [Paiute]. I made up my mind I was not going to forget my language. I knew if I did I would not be able to talk to my aunt Mary Ann. I just was not going to forget it. We wanted to talk [Paiute] so badly we would climb up in those trees. We spent a lot of time in those palm trees. We were finally told on. Someone heard us and told on us. . . . I had to scrub the bathroom. This huge bathroom. . . .

Sherman Institute Federal Indian Boarding School,
with palm trees into which Viola and her cousin Evelyn
climbed in order to speak Paiute without getting caught.
Courtesy of Sherman Institute.

Showers and bowls and toilet seats. Our assistant matron
made us clean every inch. We really learned that we
shouldn't talk Indian, but we didn't stop. . . . I was always
punished. . . . Of course you couldn't clean the toilets all the
time. But the hall needed cleaning. The hall was always in
need. . . . I just made up my mind I was never going to forget
[Paiute]. . . . Of course, eventually, we did stop [speaking
Paiute] because our life was so involved in getting the education and doing the things we were supposed to do, and we
didn't have the opportunity to talk [Paiute.][22]

Viola returned home to Owens Valley only once in twelve
years, the trip to accompany the body of her niece, the daughter
of one of her much older brothers. The loss of her native

language became painfully real when she arrived in Owens Valley and had trouble understanding her relatives, who were speaking to her in Paiute. At first she thought it was because they were speaking the Mono Lake dialect. "Later I realized I wasn't understanding any of it." This was her first real awareness in four years at Sherman Institute of her language loss.[23]

This loss and other assaults on her identity could have easily fulfilled Stonequist's criteria for creating a marginal personality. Viola's observations, however, provide deeper insight into the margin in which she found herself. When she realized she was losing her native language, she excelled in English. She determined, "If I didn't learn anything else, I was going to learn [to use] English perfectly."[24] Recent scholarship has recognized that the knowledge acquired in boarding schools, although forced, was sometimes intensely motivating.[25] Viola developed a virtually insatiable thirst for learning. "I read an awful lot. Every chance I had, I read."[26] Reading extensively raised provocative questions. She remembers wondering, "How come my brain is different from a white person's brain?"[27]

Like Thomas Jefferson Morgan, Capt. Richard H. Pratt of the U.S. Army devoted much of his life to "civilizing" Indians. Following active service in the so-called Indian wars on the southern plains, Pratt experimented with educating Indian prisoners at Fort Marion in Saint Augustine, Florida. Inspired by the success of this effort, he secured the sanction of the federal government to establish the Carlisle Indian Industrial School in Pennsylvania. Carlisle, which became the model for future Indian boarding schools, was founded on the philosophy that if Indian children were removed from their parents and sent to boarding schools far from home, they could be forced to abandon their Indian ways.[28]

Pratt created an uncompromising program of immersing Indian children in white civilization.[29] This immersion included the practice of "outing," in which children were placed as servants with white families. Pratt claimed that the outing system "breaks down their old prejudices against the whites, [their] superstition and savagery, because ... such qualities that may have grown up with them in their tribes fall in innocuous desuetude." The outing system, he argued, also ended the prejudice of the white race. "The whites learn that Indians can become useful men."[30] The Carlisle model of outing spread to other boarding schools and with it the conviction that Indians were suitable for menial labor.[31]

Although the Indian Office pushed for expansion of the outing system to the western "frontier," Pratt was opposed to extending the outing system to boarding schools in the west because, as the program was adopted in new locations, it was diverted from its original purpose. Superintendents of the western schools reported having trouble getting housewives to turn loose their Indian girls for the fall school term. Sherman Institute was struggling to keep whites from trying to exploit the outing system as a source of cheap labor. Adams notes the hypocrisy in the outing system. "Sherman boys were sent out to southern California ranches to harvest cantaloupes and oranges, [laboring] monotonously in the hot sun from daybreak to sunset ... never seeing the inside of a Victorian parlor, let alone being taken in as members of a middle-class family."[32] Nevertheless, the system expanded westward and by the early 1900s was an integral structure in the westernmost schools.

Historian Robert A. Trennert contends that the outing system, "virtually ignored" by scholars, can provide an insight into the forces governing federal Indian programs.[33] The insight is imperfect, he believes, because "very few comments of Indian students have survived."[34] The memories of Viola Martinez and Clara Moorhead Moran, her friend of seventy-four years since they met at Sherman Institute in 1927, add significantly to the literature on boarding schools.

Clara has mixed feelings about her outing experiences. She remembers a husband and wife who were "nice ... real nice," although the woman was an alcoholic and Clara's job was to curtail her drinking while the husband was away. "I was told I could get her maybe a six-pack, but not to get any more than that. . . . I don't know how she got it, but sometimes he'd go around searching and he would find empty liquor bottles, not beer, liquor, the hard stuff. I guess maybe that's why I was there, to watch her so that she didn't fall down and break her neck."[35]

Adams contends that there was something to be gained by Indian students from their outing experiences. They were able to earn money, they acquired habits of discipline, and significantly, they learned something about the marginal status imposed on Indians by white society.

Clara accepted the situation with the alcoholic employer because she found it more tolerable than her previous outing experience. She had quit that job for two reasons. "Mrs. Breen [the employer] wanted me to go to school . . . to learn how to gourmet cook. She had two daughters and two sons. Everyday I had to cook for the whole bunch of them . . . [but] she wanted me to learn gourmet cooking. . . . They had just moved into this new house. It was a great big mansion, that colonial style with the pillars. I think they were probably getting ready for parties. They needed me to cook fancy food. I didn't want to, so I quit. . . . There was something else too. I would rest everyday. I couldn't wander away, but I could rest for an hour or so. My room was right off the kitchen. . . . I could hear this noise outside my door, and I wondered what it was. I kept hearing it, and I got up and opened the door. The old man was peeking in the keyhole at me. That's why I quit, too."[36]

The terms of Clara's employment did allow her to quit a job simply by calling outing supervisors at Sherman Institute and telling them she did not like the job, without having to provide reasons. She also liked being able to earn her own money on outing jobs. "I spent it mostly on clothes. If we went to parties, we could wear the clothes we bought."[37]

The outing system at Sherman Institute, as experienced by Viola, was both an assault on her identity and an affirmation of her potential. During her first outing experience, Viola overheard a school matron declare to a prospective employer, "This is what we train them for, to take care of other people's houses and toilets."[38] She recalls her distress: "I thought [the matron] was a nice lady. I thought she even cared for us. [After that] I hated her."[39]

She relates another demoralizing outing experience with a family in San Bernardino:

> [They] were awfully nice to me; they really were. [But] at the end of summer when I went back to school, apparently a wristwatch was missing, and they just assumed that I had taken it.... I went into my room [at school] and the matron was stacking my things on the bed. When I asked her what she was doing, she said: "You are going to have to let me go through your things.... You took Mr...." I don't remember the name. She said, "You took his watch and we want it now." When she did not find the watch, the matron asked me to give her the pawn ticket. I had no idea what a pawn ticket was. I had never heard of such a thing. But she kept on saying, "You know what a pawn ticket is. You went into San Bernardino [to pawn the watch]. We will have to have a meeting with them [the employers]." That never occurred. I remember her saying, "You'll never go outing again." I stayed quiet about it because I didn't want anyone to know that I had been accused of stealing. Then a year later, they were calling names of those who were going to go outing. Doggone, if they didn't call my name.... They just made out like it was nothing, it never happened.[40]

Seriously wounded by the overheard insult and the accusation of theft, Viola could have retreated into the confines of marginality. However, she was able to discriminate between the attitudes of the two matrons and those of most of her outing employers. "The majority were wonderful people. I guess I tried awfully hard to please and do a good job. I kept saying to myself, 'If you do something, do it well.' I think this goes back to my aunt telling me, 'If you are going to do something, you do it right the first time. Don't waste any time.' Of course, this was in Indian what she was saying. It certainly stuck with me."[41]

Viola reports that she went outing every summer of her years at Sherman Institute. Emboldened by one employer's encouragement, Vi asked her if she believed that Indian girls were only good for taking care of other people's toilets. The woman's shocked response and subsequent support were a turning point for Vi. "She encouraged me. She kept telling me: 'You have a good mind.'" On later outings with other employers, she asked if it would be possible to get books from the library. "I spent my evenings reading. That was the outing program as I remember it. And that is where I got the idea that I had a brain just like anybody else. And what I did with it was up to me."[42]

In addition to babysitting, cooking, and cleaning, Vi learned to do light bookkeeping. "I didn't spend my days working and my nights sleeping there. I spent my evenings reading. . . . I took advantage of all the summers. I went to parks, to museums, and everything."

Viola recalls that in the beginning of her years at Sherman Institute, "I was always trying to see ways where I could be like a white girl, because they were the ones that were going places, becoming teachers, doing different things. The matrons would tell you, 'You are just going to have to live like a white person. You have to forget the way you were brought up because you are in a different place now. This is where you have to learn to live.'"[43]

Despite her wish to be like the white girls, she very soon began to question the indoctrination.[44] "I read an awful lot. Anything I read, I would try to see why they thought we should learn this. Sometimes in my mind I would say, 'I don't have to learn this.'" Conversely, she was determined to prove she could master "white" accomplishments, such as playing the piano. "What was different about me that I couldn't do what the person who is not brown colored was able to do? . . . I was constantly having to show myself that being Indian didn't make me any different from the person that wasn't Indian. The difference lay in what I would do with my ability. . . . If it weren't for Sherman, I wouldn't be where I am today. If it weren't for all the problems I had learning, I wouldn't have wondered, 'How come my brain is different from a white person's brain?' And then making up my mind that I was going to prove myself to those people who thought my brain was different because I was brown and they were white."[45]

Detail from photo on page 77.

4

The Creative Margin

VIOLA BELIEVES THAT THE SEED OF HER INDEPEN-
dent stance germinated on the return trip following her niece's funeral. She recognized that she no
longer quite fit in Owens Valley, nor did she fit
comfortably in Riverside. She was on the margin of
each society, partly in and partly out. During that
long train ride she realized that she needed to be in
command of this marginality. "From that point on,
whatever I did I would have to do for myself."[1]

Interviews with women who had attended St.
Benedict's Indian boarding school at White Earth,
Minnesota, between 1909 and 1945, revealed that
the school was their home—for better or for
worse.[2] Certainly, for Viola, who had no visitors,
not even a letter, from home during her five years at
Sherman Institute, the boarding school became her
home. "I wondered how long I would be away
[from Owens Valley]. In fact, I wondered if I would
ever go back. I was told by the faculty that I would
probably be better off if I just thought about going
out and working [as a domestic] in homes eventually."[3] Yet she continued to question: "Why is it that

[skin] color makes such a difference?" And she continued to be alert to opportunities to test her evolving convictions.

Some Indian students took advantage of their perceived choices, adopting some aspects of acculturation and rejecting others.[4] Because Viola recognized a choice where other Indian girls at Sherman had not, a momentous opportunity arose for her in 1932. Upon graduation from Sherman Institute, the boys were allowed to attend Riverside Polytechnic High School because they played football. "It was an impossible thing as far as girls were concerned. We never even expected to be bold enough to ask. We just assumed that [attending the high school] would never happen." But Viola wondered, "How come?"

She and her friends Eunice Lynn, a Ute, and Griselda Young, a Wintun, explored the idea of attending the non-Indian school in Riverside. "Eunice and Griselda had parents to go to. They could go home. My aunt and I had been separated for so long I felt I didn't have anyone. I decided that I was going to have to do something. I wanted someone to do it with; I just kept talking to them about trying to attend the high school in Riverside. We finally decided: 'Hey, okay, let's do it. Let's see what we can do.'"[5]

They approached Donald H. Biery, superintendent of Sherman Institute, and asked him what their chances were of attending Riverside Polytechnic High School. Vi relates, "He was a Mormon, and he was very, very outgoing. Nothing seemed to be out of line in his way of thinking. Although he was not sure if the Bureau of Indian Affairs would allow Indian girls to attend a public high school, he just said, 'Well, we could find out. But [meanwhile] you could go out to work.' That's what we had planned to do anyway, so we went outing."

Among the letters of recommendation in Viola's file in the National Archives are two from Sherman Institute, one from the head of the home economics department and one from the principal. Both evidently were solicited to strengthen her application for high school. The head of the home economics department states, "Viola Maroney [sic] is very adaptiable [sic] and a capable worker. Always keenly interested in her work. She has excellent health. She is a leader very considerate respectable dependable and trustworthy." No signature. The principal declares, "Viola Meroney, ¼ Paiute, is a good student, usually doing 'A' work. I believe that she is capable of doing college work. I have found her to be conscientious and honest. Her health is good." The letter is signed Samuel H. Gilliam, principal.

Vi tells what happened next: "Mr. Biery wrote to us and told us that we could go [to Riverside Polytechnic] to get our diploma. We ended up registering as seniors, although we lacked the solid courses for that. I had to take geometry. I had to take chemistry. I had to take English. I had to take some kind of science. . . . Gosh, we had heavy loads. And Mr. Biery was very firm, very definite. He told us we had to make straight A's. 'If you do well, we will maybe have the opportunity to help others to go.' Let me tell you, we worked hard. We had to and we did. We did."[6]

Viola's pursuit of higher education coincided with severe criticism of the boarding schools in the 1928 Meriam Report, *The Problem of Indian Administration*.[7] The report called for encouraging students to pursue higher education. When asked if she was aware of this national context, Vi said, "I really wasn't. We were being trained primarily to take care of white people's houses and I did not see any change in that emphasis."[8] Her observation is consistent with studies of the "new" government policy, which retained an emphasis on training Indians for manual labor and vocational positions.[9]

The three Indian girls from Sherman did so well in the non-Indian high school that they began to think about further education: "Gee, maybe we could go to Riverside Junior College," Vi thought. "My boyfriend, Allen Lovine, was a football star at the junior college.[10] . . . The fellas didn't have any trouble going on to junior college. So he suggested: 'Why don't you girls try and see what happens?' So we did. They checked our records, and they were at the top. So they said okay. Our grades were that good."[11] Her student record from Riverside Polytechnic High School shows all A's, with a notation "honor roll for [the] year."[12]

However, Viola's classes in Riverside Junior College were considerably more difficult. She was taking eight courses and her grades show C's in organic chemistry, economics, and chemistry. However, someone had noted on this record "very good."[13]

Biery, in a letter to Ruth M. Bronson, placement and guidance officer for the Indian Field Service of the Bureau of Indian Affairs, reported on the three girls: "Viola, who made such fine grades last year has again repeated her good work." There is no information on the academic performance of Eunice and Griselda in this letter, but Biery does report, "Eunice, Viola and Griselda each earned approximately fifteen dollars during the vacation period."[14] In a letter six months later Viola and Eunice receive from Biery nearly identical evaluations: "Eunice Lynn— Good student, very much interested in college, conduct at Sherman good. Recommendation—should return to Riverside Junior College." Viola's evaluation differs only in that she is described as a *very* good student. Griselda, however, is characterized as ambivalent: "We can't get any definite decisions from her. She is not enthused over college, and yet she says she wants to go on. . . . Recommendation—should return to Riverside Junior College if no other plan is feasible."[15] She did return and subsequently went on to college with Eunice and Vi.

While attending Riverside Junior College, the three girls worked assisting the dormitory matrons at Sherman Institute. The girls' adviser wrote a letter of recommendation for Viola, which was addressed to the commissioner of Indian affairs and reflects that Vi was gaining command of the margin in which she was living. "I can recommend her quite sincerely. Her record at high school has been superior in every respect; she has proved her ability to go ahead in a college course. She is also unusually prepossessing in appearance and charming in manner. I believe that Miss Meroney gives promise of becoming a real leader among her race."[16]

Bronson also wrote to Vi while she was attending Riverside Junior College. Bronson was a resolute advocate for higher education for Indian students during John Collier's twelve-year tenure as commissioner of Indian affairs.[17] She had obtained a small scholarship for Viola from the Indian Field Service and wrote to her the following:

> On the whole we are very much pleased with this record. If you are able to maintain this scholarship average throughout your college course, we will certainly have no cause to feel disappointed with your achievement. We hope, however, that you will be able to improve the good record you have established. Why not set for yourself the goal of eliminating the grade of C from all your future records?
>
> We are sure you could raise your average, with just a little extra work, and we are very anxious to have our scholarship students make excellent scholastic showing. You know, you really have it in your power to prove, to a sometimes doubting world, that Indians are just as capable of doing good academic work as anyone else. You have helped to prove this, very materially, by the good work you have already done, and that is one reason I want you to work hard to make a brilliant showing."[18]

Upon graduation from junior college, Viola was assured of being accepted at Bacone College in Muskogee, Oklahoma, but this was a considerable distance from her home.[19] Viola preferred a university in California. "I wanted to be close enough so that if I had the opportunity, I could go home to Owens Valley. I wanted to do that."[20]

While at junior college, Viola also worked for the Biery family on weekends. Viola asked Mrs. Biery, "Would it be all right, do you think, if I asked Mr. Biery if maybe we three girls could go to UCLA?" She explains that she asked about UCLA "because I didn't know about any other college. I had just heard about

UCLA and thought maybe that would be place we could go." When Mrs. Biery encouraged her, Viola asked Mr. Biery about the possibility of UCLA, and he promised to look into it.[21]

When the prospect became promising Vi, Lynn and Griselda toured UCLA. Vi declared: "I don't want to go here. . . . There are just too many people. I want to be where it's smaller." With the help of Donald Biery and Ruth Bronson, the three young women were admitted to Santa Barbara State College, now the University of California at Santa Barbara. "It was small. It was up on the hill. And the main thing, there were a lot of small apartments within walking distance."[22]

Meanwhile Vi's sister Winona, next oldest to her in birth order, had gone to boarding school at Stewart, Nevada. While on an outing in San Francisco she met a sailor, Ray Sherrill, whom she married. When they moved to Los Angeles, she was visited by Tom Gustie, whose wife had young relatives attending Sherman Institute. When Tom realized that Viola was alone, with no visitors, he began taking her with him on trips he made to Los Angeles with his wife's relatives. "He was a very, very loving kind of person. He really cared for the people, particularly the young people who didn't have anyone."[23]

In this way, Gustie brought Vi and Winona together again after a separation of more than ten years. The two sisters established an extremely close relationship which endured for seventy years.[24] Although she does not remember exactly how this came about, when Viola decided to enroll in Santa Barbara State College, Winona helped her financially.

Biery evidently arranged for Viola to meet John Cosgrave, a life insurance agent who established a policy for her. Cosgrave recalls the day they met:

> Her sister Winona was helping her through school. Vi was anxious to provide some security for that. This insurance policy seemed to be a way to do it. Vi came to our office in the Subway Terminal Building in Los Angeles. I told her that she would have to qualify by proving that she was insurable,

that she could pass a physical examination. So I escorted her over to the doctor's office and waited for her while she was being examined. In those days the restrictions were a little stiffer than they are today. I had all the sympathy that I could have for anybody. She was a little skinny girl, and she was working her way through school. As we walked a few blocks to the doctor's office, we had a conversation and I thought: "She has a sense of humor."[25]

Viola remembers their first meeting:

I think I was a little hesitant about being the first time in the city. I had no idea where I was supposed to go. He said I wasn't to worry, that he would be right there. . . . I realized that here was practically a stranger that cared about my feelings. [He] made a personal trip there to meet me to take me to the doctor. He did, he took me, and he cared about me. . . . For me, never having been around anyone other than government officials who were dictating to you what you should be doing and the way you should be doing it, to find that there were people who thought I was a person was very meaningful to me. He was a tall, nice-looking man, and to give time and attention to me, an Indian, meant something. . . . I think what it did for me was that it gave me the feeling I had some potential. Shucks, he was a businessman. His being nice to me was real important to me. . . . When you think about it, I had been away from home all of these years, and no one had ever come to see me. None of my own people had been able to come. The only contacts I had were people who were responsible for me. It was a job as far as they were concerned. . . . As time went on, whenever I wondered about how I was doing, was I doing all right? it just seemed that I would hear from [Cosgrave] or something would happen to bring us together. I think from that I got the idea, I can do it. I really can do it. This is making me cry.[26]

Whenever she is asked about her years at Santa Barbara State College, Vi is consistent in her response: "I was so intent on getting the requirements for the degree out of the way, I did not get involved in much else." In regard to her classes, she says, "I was eager to learn. There were not any at all I didn't like." She remembers that she especially liked cooking. "Eunice and I had a little apartment and very little money, so we had to make do with inexpensive food. We enjoyed learning how to make cheap food more appetizing."[27]

Despite their focus on study, they had boyfriends. Viola met a football player, Lauren (Larry) Bowlus, when they attended classes together. "He was Welsh—handsome man. He was a very handsome man. He wanted to marry me, but I wouldn't marry him because he was not Indian. . . . But he was my boyfriend."[28] Viola says she "took a shine to him," and they became very good friends. She and Eunice and Griselda used to double- and triple-date, almost always to athletic events. "That was our big thing. Eunice and I lived together, so we did everything together."[29] Griselda was included in virtually everything, and the threesome formed a bond that endured for a number of years following their graduation.

One particular activity Vi shared with Eunice was attending the Latter Day Saints church. Viola also explored various Protestant churches without Eunice. "Maybe someone at the college would tell me about the church they were going to. I'd say, 'Oh, I'd like to go there.'" Most often, however, she accompanied Eunice to her church.

> She was a Mormon, and she was a very good Mormon, because her parents, apparently, on the reservation became involved with the Mormon Church. There were things that she would tell me about the Mormon Church that I thought, "Gee, that sounds good. That sounds real good." The Bible became more plausible for me, I think, through some of the beliefs that she mentioned. One of the things she did tell me: "You know, they take care of their children. They make sure their children are taken care of, that they get the right training. It's very, very important to Mormons . . . the upbringing of the children." I thought that was wonderful,

because it's an Indian trait. The other thing I learned from her was that they make sure their people are fed. They make sure that the produce, whatever is cultivated, supplies their people. Isn't that the way Indians feel? . . . I did see that they did special things for the young people. They [also] did special things for the old people, made sure they were taken care of. . . . So, I actually did think in terms of maybe I would like to join them. I can't really say [why I didn't]. . . . There really was nothing there that I was against. Maybe it had something to do with the marriage thing [polygamy].[30]

In her pursuit of higher education, Viola had applied for a grant from the Anna E. Peale Bequest. Notifying Vi that she had been awarded the "educational gift," Biery admonished her, "Please write to the trustees thanking them and describing how you intend to use the money." He added a last bit of authoritarian advice: "This is the end of this fund so make good use of it."[31]

Viola manifests considerable maturity in her response to Biery:

I wish to extend my appreciation to you for making the gift from the Peale Foundation possible. I appreciate everything you have done for me, and I will do my best to deserve all your kindness.

I hope Mrs. Biery and the children are well. I imagine [Biery's daughter] Joy is quite a young lady now. We surely miss you all. But we are happy here in our home and with our friends.

School is very interesting. We are both taking eight laboratory periods. And so you see we spend practically all of our time in school. We both don't mind and enjoy our work. We are taking Food and Physiological Chemistry, Secondary Education, Dress Design and Selection, Foods, Clothing Construction and Care of Household Equipment.

Thank you again for everything.[32]

In another letter to Biery she wrote: "One semester is gone and now we begin on another, a much harder one, I'm afraid.

Griselda is getting along very nicely, and we all have some happy times together. I hope everything is well with [your] family. We may see you soon, perhaps during Easter vacation." She signed the letter "Thank you, Viola Meroney."[33]

Ruth Bronson, who later retired from the BIA and became the executive director of the Legal Aid and Service Bureau of the National Congress of American Indians, is noted as being "on good terms with white reformers."[34] Her profound desire to aid as many Indian students as possible is explicit in a letter to Vi dated 24 June 1937. "This is in reference to your letter asking for educational assistance for next year. . . . Can you not get along without any further aid from our Office? As you know, our funds are limited, and we have a number of Indian students who need help but we are not able to assist. If you can get through school without the aid of the [additional] tuition grant from us, this will mean that we can help some other student this next school year."[35]

While earning her degree at Santa Barbara State College, Vi also attended Woodbury Business School to learn typing so she could do part-time office work to help with her expenses. Viola, Griselda, and Eunice, all three, were graduated in 1939, each with a bachelor of science degree in home economics and a secondary teaching credential. Vi reports that, just as they had worked and studied together, the three women celebrated together.

Vi's daughter, Vianne, expresses her profound admiration for her mother. "When I tell people I am Indian, I usually tell them about my mom, about how she went to Sherman and that she went to college. During the depression, that was very, very unusual. I think she made quantum leaps for her era."[36]

Vianne's assessment is underscored by statistics regarding Indian students more than fifty years following her mother's graduation from Santa Barbara State College. For every one hundred American Indian students entering high school, sixty will graduate. Of those, about twenty will attempt postsec-

Viola's graduation picture, Santa Barbara State College, 1939. The inscription "To my darlings with love" was to her children when she gave them copies of the photo.
Courtesy of Viola Martinez.

ondary education, and perhaps three will receive a four-year college degree.[37]

At the time Viola was pursuing a college education, the Bureau of Indian Affairs, in part due to prompting by Ruth Bronson, had initiated a major policy shift and was encouraging Indian students to seek postsecondary education.[38] When asked if she was aware of the change in policy, she responded, "I wasn't really. It was Mr. Biery who made it possible for us to go to college. In fact, I had the impression that he was not sure if the BIA would allow us girls to go to college."[39]

Following graduation, Griselda moved to San Francisco. Vi recalls that Griselda "loved cosmetology very much. She married, and I know that for a while, she set up a beauty studio."[40]

Biery wrote to Viola expressing regret that he and his wife had been unable to attend her graduation and stating that he had been informed that Eunice would be getting married in the near future in Utah and would not be seeking employment as a teacher. He advises Vi, "I hope your present work [in Los Angeles] is very interesting and worthwhile, but I personally believe that you will get far ahead in the long run if you will secure employment as a home economics teacher. It will be a fine thing for you to work in public schools for a few years and, then, later if you so desire, enter the Indian service."[41]

He urged her at least once more to enter the Indian Field Service as a teacher. In a letter dated 21 May 1940, he reminded her that he had told her about a teaching position on the Fort Yuma Indian Reservation in California and insisted that she promptly have Santa Barbara State College send her transcripts to the appropriate individuals and that she write to them herself. "In writing your letter it would be a very good thing to stress not only your training and experience in Home Ecoomics and your ability to teach the regular grammar school subjects, but also your ability to handle extra-curricular activities such as physical education, recreational activity, singing, and art work. I further suggest that you mention to them your willingness to drive down to Yuma for a personal interview."[42] Viola reports that she had no intention of driving to Yuma. She had no interest in the job. She wanted to work with her own people. "My primary thought was, eventually, I would be going to Bishop [in Owens Valley]. I had planned all along that I would return to Bishop and . . . teach my own people."

Because she and Winona had grown so close, she had decided to go to Los Angeles, where Winona was living. "First of all, to work a little bit, to see if I could have some kind of income. . . . The other thing that was good about coming into Los Angeles was I had worked in a sufficient number of homes [so] that if I couldn't do anything else . . . I could still work in homes. But my thought was that surely there was something else I could do in Los Angeles."[43]

Contrary to what Biery had heard, Eunice had not returned to Utah to get married. Rather, she and Viola moved to Los Angeles and rented an apartment together for about a year, until Vi moved in with Winona. "Eunice and I both started to look for work. I figured it was not time for me to go up home, because I didn't have anything. I had to have something to go home. I had to build up some kind of fund to do this." She and Eunice heard that there might be work for them in the welfare department in the Department of Social Services. "Apparently there was a need for social workers. I don't know how we found out about it, but we went to the welfare department and applied. We both were hired."

A car was a requirement for the job in order for Eunice and Vi to visit their clients. "Eunice knew how to drive [but] I had to learn how to drive a car."[44] Vi did not tell her prospective employers that she did not know how to drive. She called her friend Larry in Santa Barbara. "'I need your car, Larry, and you have to teach me to drive!' He said, 'What for?' I said, 'I have a job if you do this.' He said, 'Swell, that's great. I'll come down on the weekend, and we'll see what we can do.'"

Larry did come to Los Angeles that weekend to teach Vi, but Winona had her doubts: "Winona said, 'You'll never learn to drive.' She was always that way. 'Oh, you'll never learn.' But, then, when it was over she said, 'Oh, I knew you would.' That was her way of egging you on. . . . She would make you irritated enough that you would say, 'Well, doggone it, I'm going to show you! Wait and see what I'll do!'"[45]

Vi did learn how to drive that weekend. "Burbank used to be a great big wide open space where the airport is now. There was nothing out there but good roads. Not a lot of traffic, you saw a car every half hour or so. Larry taught me to drive, then loaned me his car, a Model-A Ford. He was a nice guy."[46]

Vi also tells a story about how she and a cousin, Eleanor Bethel, who had been working on an outing from Sherman Institute in a home in Beverly Hills, wanted to borrow Larry's car to go from Los Angeles to Bishop.[47] Larry agreed without a word of objection. When they got to Bishop, they decided to go on to Reno, Nevada, where there was a Labor Day Indian rodeo. They especially wanted to see Mary Ann's son, Nick Brazzanovich, a well-known rodeo performer. As they were leaving, Nick and Minnie Williams, Eleanor's mother, gave them twenty dollars each because they were worried about the young women driving alone to Los Angeles. Vi says, "Fools that we were, we didn't think we would need the money."

The radiator on the Ford developed trouble, and they continually put water in it, until they arrived in Mojave, California, where garage attendants told them they could not drive to Los Angeles with the faulty radiator. Vi recalls that the mechanics were very kind and generous in repairing the radiator. Since she does not remember a problem with money, either the relatives' gift had been enough or the garage did not charge more than they had. "And Larry got his car back, all nice and fixed."

Back in Los Angeles, her responsibilities as a social worker included going to people's homes to assess their needs. "Why they gave me the assignment I have no idea [but] it was a good thing because I enjoyed it. It was working with the blind. My caseload consisted of aid to the blind, partially self-supporting blind, and the aged."

She remembers one client in particular. "We got along beautifully. She liked me and I liked her. We had something in common.... If there was something extra, I would make extra trips for her and take her to the doctor or run errands for her. I did that with all my blind people. She had secured two baskets from a Canadian friend who was Indian. When she was no longer able to function well, she decided to go back home to be with her sister. She wanted to give me the baskets. At first I didn't want to take them. She insisted. 'I would like for you to have them because you are an Indian, and you have been good to me.' That's how I got the Canadian Indian baskets, which I treasure."[48]

Viola reviews this time, living in Southern California:

I have gone through school here, I've finished college, and now I'm working. Tom Gustie had been visiting Winona in Los Angeles. He was now up in Bishop, and the girls [whom he had visited at Sherman Institute] are in Owens Valley, starting their new families. And here I am down here still trying to find my way. Winona has started her family; she has two children now. She is having trouble with her husband.... He was a good man, but he was an alcoholic. She was trying to make up her mind whether she wants to continue to live with him. He was never unkind, but he just drank.

Who comes into the picture again? Tom.... He gets in touch with me, and he tells me about land assignments [allotments] for Paiutes in Owens Valley. He was responsible for me making the decision: why don't we go back up? I want to go up there to teach, and this is a good opportunity. We can get an assignment on the reservation. Winona, with these two kids, wanting a divorce. I can apply for a teaching job. I was so sure I was going to get it. No question in my mind. We can go up there and start new.[49]

5

Return to Owens Valley

THE ASSIGNMENTS OF LAND THAT TOM GUSTIE urged Viola and Winona to accept were like a magnet drawing the sisters home to Owens Valley. In the 1920s the city of Los Angeles, in an effort to silence opposition to its quest for water and to establish its control over Owens Valley, began buying virtually all the farms, ranches, and towns in the valley. By 1933, the city owned 95 percent of the farmland and 85 percent of non-farm property in Owens Valley. The consequent decline in economic activity was disastrous for the approximately eight hundred Paiutes living in the valley. Off-reservation employment disappeared as whites left the area; and although the Paiutes' land and water rights were under federal protection, efforts at agriculture on their nonarable lands were futile.[1]

After attempts to remove the Paiutes from Owens Valley failed, the city finally acknowledged that it had "an Indian problem." In 1937 an agreement was reached between the city of Los Angeles and the U.S. Department of the Interior that provided for a series of land exchanges establishing the Bishop, Lone Pine, and Big Pine reservations.

The agreement, enacted in 1939, provided the Owens Valley Paiutes with better lands and with water rights. The federal government built new housing and installed sewer and irrigation systems on the tracts in the early 1940s.[2]

Viola is not sure how she and Winona were listed on the tribal roll. "Because my Uncle Joe Lent spoke English, very good English, as I recall . . . he probably made sure our names were [written] down."[3] She does remember that

Tom Gustie was very eager to have Indians from Bishop be aware that they had the opportunity to request land to live on there. Many of them were not aware of how important that was. . . . The size [of the reservation] was going to be dependent on how many who were recognized as Owens Valley Indians wanted an assignment to live on. . . . Many of them just didn't understand that it was necessary for them to make a request. They just assumed it was their land. Why did they have to ask permission to come back to something that was already theirs? . . . He had to make it known to them that they had to do this, because it had to be down in black and white. It would be a piece of land that they could use forever and it would be theirs. He felt that the people that could help were those of us that understood what it meant to have this [land]. At first Winona said, "No way." She was not interested. She was taken off the reservation as a very young child; she was sent away to school, and no one had ever cared about her. . . . Up to a point, I felt the same way. Then, of course, I also realized that there were people like my aunt who didn't have anything. She had been taken up to Bridgeport by her son, because she didn't have a place in Benton. There was no place for her. I felt that if we did go up [to Owens Valley] maybe we would have an opportunity to help her. My thoughts were still: "I want to go home. I want to teach in the schools up there. This is where I want to be anyway."[4]

She succeeded in talking her sister into returning to Owens Valley. One of the first things they did was visit Aunt Mary Ann, whom Vi had not seen since she left for Sherman Institute as a young child. "She was living in Bridgeport. Her son had taken her from Benton when she was not able to take care of herself. There was a little cabin for her, across the street from his house where his family, his wife and children, lived. That's where I saw her for the first time. She didn't recognize me. I went [away] as a little girl, and here I am coming back a woman. This [remembering] is making tears come to my eyes. Oh, this is terrible."[5]

Over time they became reacquainted enough that Vi asked her aunt if she would like to come down and live in Bishop. "At that time [her son] Nick was thinking about moving to Carson.

Viola at Mary Ann's house that had been moved from Bridgeport to Winona's assignment land.
Photo by the author.

She said yes, she would like that. We moved her little house down for her." So that Viola and Winona could take care of their aunt, Mary Ann's house was placed on the allotment property, where it remains to this day.[6]

Viola recalls reconnecting with her extended family:

When we went back up to the reservation after finishing school, I became reacquainted with all of the Lents. The Lents from Benton were involved in the land acquisition. There are some Lents today that are working in Bishop. They are my cousins. We used to talk about when we were little. We were one family, because if anything happened, all of those people were there, helping, doing, making sure we were taken care of. That's the reason I mention them the way I do, because they are my family.

I was very close to Earl Lent when we moved up to Bishop. His mother, Mabel Lent, was one of the people that was in Los Angeles at the time that Tom Gustie would come to the school and invite me to go visit the family in Los Angeles. She was working in Los Angeles. [Later] Earl Lent did get an assignment fairly close to ours. We still keep in touch with him whenever we can. . . . And I know that his children are involved in the reservation business there. . . .[7]

As for my uncles, none of them really had had a great deal to do with how I was raised, because my aunt took care of me all of those first years, and then I was at school and away the rest of the time. When I did go back to Owens Valley, they were all deceased except for Uncle Bob [Somerville]. I have the feeling that when Winona and I moved up there he made the effort to get reacquainted with us because we were taking care of Aunt Mary Ann then. It was a natural thing for him to come around.

Of course, I latched on to him real fast. I like his ways. He was very, very friendly. He never acted mysterious. If you wanted to find out anything, he gave you answers that you could accept. Very definitely open about things. He seemed to be very self-sufficient. He seemed to be able to handle himself well in any situation. He was willing to try new things. He loved going out looking for gold and silver. It was a big thing. He was well known by the white people [in the] Tonopah and the Hawthorne [Nevada] area. He was a prospector, and he did well as a prospector. As I said before, I think my aunt was helped by him occasionally.[8]

Bob Somerville continued to be a large presence in the lives of Viola and her family.

Vi realized she had truly returned to her homeland and her family when she and Winona and Winona's two children, Richard and Alberta Sherrill, were given a family allotment with a three-bedroom house, based on the size of the family.[9] "The houses were supplied [by the federal government]. A standard-issue house. . . . They provided the utilities and a barn and an outside toilet. Why that was provided I don't know, because we had a bathroom inside."

"Each person was allowed two acres. Each person with a family was allowed two acres and an acre home site. . . . In our case, there were four of us. We had eight acres plus the home site. . . . When Tom brought the map to us and said, 'These are the vacant spots. . . . Where would you like to be?' Of course when I saw Bishop Creek, I said, 'Hey, let's go fishing!' It's a beautiful parcel."[10]

Viola says with pride: "I helped build the barn. Put the roof on. It's still there. Winona says, 'You did a good job.' We bought a milk cow. We bought chickens. We built a little enclosure near the house so we could have our chicken coop there. We built fences around the barn. We had a horse. The rest of the land we planted in corn. We thought that would sell well. We [also] sold the eggs, and we sold the milk."

"When we went up, Winona immediately went out looking for work, and she found a job working in a laundry [in Bishop]." Viola applied for a teaching job in Bishop. "I was told they were not hiring Indians, because 'the people don't want an Indian teaching white students.'" Characteristically, her response to this humiliating disappointment was to apply immediately for a

Winona's house built on her assignment land in Bishop (ca. 1996).
Photo by the author.

different job. "Because I needed work and because I felt that I
had the knowledge, I applied for office manager of the Bishop
Indian agency and I got it. . . . It was just about the time I
married Andy."[11]

Viola relates how she met Andrew Martinez:

We both attended Sherman Indian School [at different
times], and we both have relatives in Bishop. We're both
Paiutes. We had mutual friends. In fact, I met his half-
brother in Los Angeles at a Christmas affair. This man who
was the one who arranged for me to come to Los Angeles for
Christmas, Tom Gustie, was Andy's uncle. . . . I knew of
Andy. He was a very nice-looking man. Handsome man.
Tall. I'd heard of him because he had friends who spoke
highly of him. I didn't meet Andy at Sherman or in Los
Angeles. I met him later on when we moved to Bishop. . . .
He, of course, came to visit his relatives. That's when we got

acquainted. We eventually eloped to Las Vegas. Yes, we eloped. We just all of a sudden decided to get married. This was in 1942.[12]

Andy, who had acquired carpentry skills at Sherman Institute, was working as a carpenter in Bishop just before he was called to the war. Andy and Viola had moved into an empty home on the reservation. "One of the families had been given an assignment and had to go away to work. They rented their home to us, just temporarily. When Andy went into the service, I moved back with my sister."

Meanwhile Winona became involved with Clyde Roach, an electrician whom she later married. Vi recalls a project of theirs:

> He had friends that would come up [to Owens Valley] with trailers and would need places to stay and camp. He suggested [to Winona] that they have some kind of setup so they could have trailers. The tribe had the right to decide how the people would handle their assignments so that they were not encroaching on one another. The government was concerned about seeing that eligible Indians in that valley did have a piece of land, and it had to be surveyed . . . it was all according to law. . . . I understood that the only thing we had to make sure of was making good use of the land.
>
> [Winona and Clyde] worked together on establishing a trailer camp. A couple of groups came up and wanted a place for the summer. They had trailers. . . . A couple of them asked [Winona] if they could stay [on her property]. She decided, "Yes, for a little while." It got to be such a nice idea that she finally asked me, "What do you think about it?" I said, "Do it! That's your acreage. Use it for whatever you want." There were many areas nearby where people had trailer parks [but] she was the first one on the reservation. . . . I don't think they expected it to work out to be as good a thing as it did.[13]

Winona had been augmenting the family income by renting space to mobile-home owners since 1942. When she suffered a severe stroke in 1995, her daughter Alberta, called Sussi by the family, assumed management of the allotment property.

During the 1940s, Winona worked in the laundry in Bishop and Vi worked for the Indian Field Service Agency until an opportunity arose for a job with the Federal Housing Authority (FHA) in Bishop and Pine Creek. Andy encouraged Vi to apply, but she demurred. "They wouldn't want me." However, when Andy was drafted, Vi realized she didn't want "to stay on the reservation with this little job," meaning her job with the Indian Agency.

I don't know how long he had been gone when I finally applied. My husband's uncle Tom said: "Do it." So I went and applied and never expected to get it, and doggone it, I got it. ... Manager of the housing project. A big shot! Head of the whole thing! The chamber of commerce in Bishop didn't like it, because they thought that the job would go to a non-Indian. They were sure it would be a non-Indian, and it would be a man.

These were houses for anyone that had jobs up in that area. They were putting in highways. They were working up in the mines. There were all kinds of war-related jobs in that area. But there was no housing. ... It was a very demanding job. ... We handled the renting, the upkeep, you know, the maintenance. ... The renters were all white, because the Indians had their own houses now on the reservation.

My workers also were all white. And that was interesting, because when we would need someone to come in to do the digging and the menial kind of labor . . . that was the only time that I found that I wouldn't get people that were industrious enough and wanted to work. I always seemed to get all the bums. They would send people that nobody else would use, I guess. They just didn't want me to do well, I think.

I would go to the Department of Labor downtown [in Bishop]. It was hard for me to realize that they were not cooperating. It wasn't a matter of opposition, they just didn't cooperate.... Here I am an Indian, a woman. [And their attitude was] I didn't know how to handle the men. I didn't know how to handle the crew I had. . . . It was very subtle. But it just seemed that I always had trouble. And if I did go out on my own and find people, I did better.[14]

While she was employed by the FHA she had a visit from John Cosgrave. He recalls a visit with her: "I was coming back from Utah and I had heard that she was there [in Bishop]. . . . I stopped to talk with her, and she introduced me to some friends of hers that I did business with, sold policies to. She then told me what she was doing. . . . She had lifted herself up by the bootstraps and she did the job very well. She was conscientious and made a great success out of that. I was exploded with pride when I learned that she had an important job as manager of a government housing project. I thought that was great. I was so proud of her that I burst my buttons."[15]

Viola anticipated the end of the FHA job and prepared for it.

When we realized that the war was coming to an end, many people would be moving and wouldn't be needing the houses. That was something that was going to happen. My husband was still in the service and I didn't want to leave Bishop. I needed a job.

A white man named Clyde Raymond, an insurance agent, always came around to visit Winona and me because he had heard about these two Indian women who had an assignment on the reservation and were farming it. We planted corn and raised chickens. We were going to do what they said we were supposed to do, use the land to make a living. We were using it to feed us, my sister, my niece and nephew. He said it tickled him to think of two Indian women out there doing that. Of course, he was trying to sell insurance, too. I don't know what struck him about me, but he took a shine to me. Any time that he saw me, he always made a point of talking to me, treating me like an equal. When I went to work for the housing project, he always made a point of stopping by, checking up on me, making sure things were okay. Naturally, I suppose he would go all up and down

Owens Valley. He found out that they were looking for help [at Manzanar]. I had mentioned that I was going to have to be looking for something. He suggested that I go down there. That's how I came to apply and I ended up there at Manzanar.[16]

An unlikely place for Paiute Indians, Euro-Americans, and Japanese Americans to converge: Manzanar—550 windswept, arid acres between the towns of Lone Pine and Independence in Owens Valley.

6

Converging Paths
Native Americans, Euro-Americans, and Japanese Americans at Manzanar

Executive Order 9066

Now, therefore, by virtue of the authority vested in me as President of the United States and Commander-in-Chief of the Army and Navy, I hereby authorize and direct the Secretary of War and the Military Commanders whom he may from time to time designate, whenever he or any designated Commander deems such action necessary or desirable, to prescribe military areas in such places and of such extent as he or the appropriate Military Commander may determine, from which any or all persons may be excluded, and with respect to which, the right of any person to enter, remain in, or leave shall be subject to whatever restrictions the Secretary of War or the appropriate Military Commander may impose in his discretion.

Franklin D. Roosevelt
19 February 1942[1]

Executive Order 9066, issued seventy-four days after the Japanese attack on Pearl Harbor, was an unprecedented and absolute delegation of presidential authority to a subordinate. Although there was no direct mention of Japanese Americans, the authority was used only against people of Japanese ancestry residing on the West Coast.[2] On 2 March 1942, Gen. John L. DeWitt, western defense commander, based in San Francisco, issued an order directing that all persons of Japanese ancestry, defined as individuals with a percentage of Japanese blood of one thirty-second or more, be removed from the western portion of Washington, Oregon, California, and southern Arizona. A new civilian agency, the War Relocation Authority (WRA), was created by Executive Order 9102 on 18 March 1942 to develop removal plans for the people excluded from the military areas. The transfer of the excluded population began in March and continued through November 1942.[3] A total of 112,581 Japanese Americans, primarily American citizens, were interred in ten "relocation" centers.[4] Manzanar, one of the ten centers, is the site on which the federal government, during one of the most painful episodes in U.S. history, detained behind barbed wire and beneath guard towers 10,046 Japanese Americans, most of whom were American citizens.

There has been considerable controversy regarding terminology related to the camps.[5] The WRA coined euphemisms to avoid the reality of the internment of United States citizens under the guise of military necessity. The board of the Civil Liberties Public Education Fund (CLPEF) has issued guidelines regarding this terminology. The CLPEF discourages the use of euphemisms such as "evacuation" and "relocation centers." It suggests, instead, the use of "imprisonment," "detention," or "incarceration" for "evacuation" or "relocation"; and "internment camp" or even "concentration camp" for "relocation center." The National Park Service, which has overseen the administration of Manzanar since its designation as a National Historic Site in February 1985, has objected to the use of "concentration camp" because of the term's association with the Nazi death camps. After extensive debate, it was decided that the wording on the commemorative plaque at Manzanar National Historic Site would use only the term "relocation center," although the plaque for the California State Historic Site includes "concentration camp." Both plaques will be on display when the site is completed.[6]

Basic construction of the camp at Manzanar, which encompassed 6,000 acres, began in March 1942 and was completed in six weeks, primarily with Japanese American labor. In addition to 550 acres for living quarters for detainees and employees, the camp included a reservoir, a hospital, and a cemetery. By August 1942, Manzanar also had eight watch towers, a five-strand barbed wire fence, and a military police compound.[7]

The first 82 Japanese Americans traveled by bus 220 miles from Los Angeles to Manazar on 21 March 1942. By mid-April, approximately 1,000 detainees were arriving each day. By July the camp had a population of nearly 10,000, over 90 percent of whom were from the Los Angeles area. Others were relocated from Stockton, California, and Bainbridge Island, Washington.[8]

Partially due to the wartime labor shortage, the WRA encountered siginficant difficulties in recruiting administrative staff for Manzanar during its entire existence. Although Robert Brown, assistant project director of Manzanar, estimates that perhaps as high as 50 percent of the administrators of the war relocation centers came from the Bureau of Indian Affairs, research has not substantiated this claim.[9]

The National Park Service has identified four employees with Indian heritage who worked at Manzanar, one of whom is Viola Martinez. Vi, however, distinctly remembers relatives who were not identified, although they worked at the camp. Lawrence Van Horn, cultural anthropologist for the National Park Service, conducted an ethnographic assessment for the proposed Manzanar National Historic Site in 1995. From interviews with local Indian people he has surmised that a considerable number had worked on constructing Manzanar and on dismantling the camp after the war. He concludes, "Employment at the war relocation center figures into the Paiute and Shoshone ties to Manzanar and may be considered part of the Owens Valley Indian identity."[10]

Because of her education and experience Vi was hired as a counselor in 1945 by Walter A. Heath, who held various titles such as leave officer, assistant relocation officer, relocation program officer, and relocation officer, but essentially directed the re-relocation program during its entire existence, which began as early as 1942.[11]

Caucasian staff living quarters, Manzanar relocation camp. The Manzanar Committee requested that both "relocation center" and "concentration camp" be included on the commemorative plaque designating the site a historic landmark. The request was granted by the state, but the National Park Service uses only "relocation center" on its plaque. Both plaques will be on display when the site is completed. Courtesty of Eastern California Museum.

According to Heath, this program, which was initially designed to relocate internees outside the area of the western defense command, required the counselors to "exert the greatest of patience, understanding, and skill."[12] Viola recalls, "They would relocate them into areas like . . . Idaho, Utah . . . but they didn't let them get too close to the ocean."[13]

In her work Vi used a newly designed form entitled "Application for Permit to Leave a Relocation Center for Private Employment," which elicited information about relatives, residence, education, references, activities, and hobbies. Additional notes were taken on the "degree of Americanization." Viola states it succinctly: "The main thing that they wanted us to make sure of was that they definitely would not be disloyal." She adds, "Really, I had no idea how to do that. I was told that we want them to understand that they are being sent inland rather than to the coast. They said, 'Get an expression from them how they feel about this.' . . . Many of them didn't like it; they felt there were other ways this could have been taken care of."[14]

As the wartime labor shortage reached western agricultural areas, employment opportunities for internees outside the camps increased significantly.[15] Vi recalls that the majority of those she counseled, even in early 1945, were relocated again, this time from Manzanar onto ranches and farms. "The majority of them, we were told, were wonderful gardeners. . . . Working for ranches, they could probably help in supplying food."[16]

According to the War Relocation Authority, nearly half of the relocated workers in 1943 were in agriculture or domestic service. Others were engaged in occupations ranging from unskilled labor to technical and professional work.[17] Viola recalls that there were opportunities for work as "hairdressers and things of that sort. . . . And a lot of them went into health and nursing."[18]

Heath reported that many internees at Manzanar were deeply rooted in the California communities from which they had been evacuated. They would say with emotion that Santa

Monica was their home. When the war had ended they refused employment and housing in any but the exact location of their pre-evacuation residence.[19] When they encountered difficulties in returning to their homes, Viola recalls, "They were very unhappy about it. This is where they [had] lived, and this is there they [had] made their living. The area that later on I realized was one of their favorites was the area here where I live," in West Los Angeles, bordering on Santa Monica.

While Viola was fully engaged in employment counseling of the Japanese Americans at Manzanar, her life in the Paiute community continued. Aunt Mary Ann became ill. "She was doing poorly," says Vi. "So I went up [to Bishop]. There was no way I could leave her. Winona and I felt it would be better for her to be with me at Manzanar. . . . I could check on her regularly and have some of the Japanese [American] people come in and check on her. I figured she would be more comfortable. . . . We didn't realize how bad she was. . . . I put her to bed and was with her that evening. She died during the night." She reports that Mary Ann's death caused no problems with Manzanar authorities. "We [Indians] were our own bosses for a change."[20]

Grace Washington, who later became the wife of Vi's cousin Harry Keller, worked at Manzanar with Vi. Grace, called Little Auntie by the family, had lost her first husband in a mining accident and was a single mother of two-year-old Gilbert while she was working at the camp. She worked nights as a telephone operator, while Vi worked days, so they could share the care of Gilbert. Although Grace also had a Japanese American girl helping to care for Gilbert, he somehow "escaped" the compound and was found on the highway by the police, who reported that a little Japanese boy was in the middle of the highway and someone should come and get him. Viola realized it was probably Gilbert and rescued him.[21]

Vi tells of another incident at Manzanar, which for fifty years has made a great family story: "They did hire Indians to work at Manzanar. They worked in the shops. Some were carpenters.

Some worked out in the fields. I don't know what Uncle Tom [Gustie] was doing there at the time, but he was working. They would check them in at the gates, and when they left in the evening, they would check them out. They all had to show their [identification] tags." She quotes her uncle-in-law, "We started off [toward the exit gate] and all of a sudden this car came up behind us, blowing the horn and telling us to stop. They stopped us because they thought I was a Japanese trying to escape." Vi says that only Gustie was suspect. "The rest looked Indian, I guess. . . . I wasn't even aware he was working there, but I did say to [the authorities] that he was my husband's uncle. . . . Uncle Tom used to laugh about that. He thought that was really funny. He used to say: "I never should have told them. I could have lived there and not had to work. They brought the Japanese up here and fed them and everything. They never fed us."

Viola, however, has a different view. She recognized qualities in the internees similar to those that had enabled her to take advantage of perceived choices while in boarding school. "I thought the Japanese [Americans] were fine people. It struck me too that here were people from the big city taken and put out [far] away from the city. Not because they wanted to go. Not even a question about whether they would like to go."[22]

The Japanese [Americans] from what I could see . . . their way of doing things was just unbelievable. Nothing was left to chance. They had an idea of what they were doing. They seemed to know this is the way they needed to direct their resources. They had a purpose in life, and it had to be a way that was going to be of worth to them as a people.[23]

I remember one lady. She was very, very talented in a number of things. But the thing that she could do exceptionally well was crocheting and needlepoint. She was excellent. . . . She did everything that she could to get the materials she needed to work with [and] to find a place in which to work. Just her way of using the resources and using her ability. Just very, very definite, knowing what she was doing was going to be good, going to be worthwhile.[24]

Ansel Adams, one of America's finest landscape photographers, attempted to document the internment experience at Manzanar. His photographs suggest the values to which Viola refers. Forbidden by the camp director, Robert Merritt, to photograph the guard towers, guards, or barbed wire, Adams used his photos to depict the successful adaptation of the Japanese Americans to life in the camp. A major emphasis in his photos was the impact of the Owens Valley landscape on the life and spirit of the internees.[25]

Vi remembers fleeting glimpses of Adams. "He was coming and going constantly; he was constantly taking pictures. I thought that was something crazy. . . . He would be there for awhile, then all of a sudden he would be gone. Then he would come back. . . . I didn't have sense enough to realize what a wonderful person he was. . . . He was there [in the camp] taking pictures, and he was going up into the mountains taking pictures. All around the area taking pictures. We didn't have sense enough to know we had a treasure [in him]. . . . I have a copy of *Born Free and Equal*. I made a point of keeping it, because I felt that it would be very important one day."[26]

In the *First Quarterly Report* of the War Relocation Authority evacuee employment was delineated. The WRA had early determined that each detention camp should "be as nearly self-sufficient as possible." Agricultural potential was considered in locating the camps, so that the internees could produce food needed for the community. Manzanar very quickly set up a hog farm, a chicken ranch, and vegetable gardens. There were government-sponsored projects to produce articles needed by the internees, such as clothing. Detainees were employed in all phases of the building and maintenance of the camp.[27]

Viola's observations echo the WRA report. "They certainly maintained a well-kept place. They were definitely interested in keeping on with the education programs for the children. They had to maintain the barracks. They had to have food. So what did they do? They had the fields plowed, and they grew vegetables and grains. . . . They did the cooking, the laundry, and all of that for the people who were living there."[28]

Perhaps Viola's most provocative observation is the comparison she draws between Sherman Institute and Manzanar. About Sherman Institute she remembers, "We [children] ran the school. . . . You learned to cook. You washed, you ironed. . . . You did the sewing and you did the cleaning. The boys . . . learned to do the electrical work. . . . And the farming. They went out and dug the big farm. . . . They provided the necessary labor so that we had good food. All those things. . . . [The federal government] had it worked out so that by doing all of these things you got a well-rounded education, if that's what you want to call it."[29]

Viola underscores the parallel between the federal Indian boarding schools and the World War II federal internment camps. "Here is the situation. . . . People are put into a position where they have to feed themselves, clothe themselves, house themselves, even educate themselves, in a sense."[30]

Vi discerned other parallels in her interactions with Japanese Americans at Manzanar. She remembers an internee asking her about Indians. "I had that kind of relationship with her," Vi explains, "and she was very interested." Vi recalls the young woman saying, "Well, in a way, the government has taken from you like they are doing to us."[31]

The U.S. Supreme Court eventually ruled on the constitutional issues involved in the detention of Japanese Americans. In two cases, *Hirabayashi v. United States* (21 June 1943) and *Korematsu v. United States* (18 December 1944), the Court upheld the government's right to enforce curfews and to exclude people of Japanese ancestry from the West Coast due to military necessity. In the third case, however, *Endo v. United States,* the court ruled, also on 18 December 1944, that the government did not have the right to confine loyal Japanese Americans. This ruling, in effect, released all Japanese Americans from the relocation centers.[32]

Anticipating Supreme Court decisions favorable to the

detainees, on 17 December 1944 the WRA rescinded the West Coast exclusion orders and announced that the camps would be closed within a year. Initial response by Japanese Americans ranged from immediate return to the West Coast to refusal to leave the camps.[33] The reaction by many Manzanar detainees to the WRA's announced intention to close the camps was "marked apathy."[34]

Viola describes the mood in the camp when the war ended: "It was interesting. I don't know whether it was because they felt they couldn't show elation. . . . It was hard to tell because you didn't hear them vocalize much on this. You never knew just how they really felt. Now what they said to other people, I have no idea. They probably were more vocal among themselves."[35]

The last six months of the WRA were relatively quiet, with the remaining staff members working on liquidation and final reports.[36] When the war ended, Vi went into the main office at Manzanar. "We started a form of dismantling. I had gone to Woodbury College to learn bookkeeping, so I ended up [at Manzanar] helping them to close the place. It seemed to me it took maybe a half a year. We closed out accounts, closed out a lot of things."[37]

Congruent with Van Horn's findings that many Paiutes and Shoshones found work in helping to dismantle Manzanar, Vi's husband Andy returned to Owens Valley, upon completing his military service, and was immediately hired as a carpenter at the camp. Vi says, "When he came out of the service, naturally he came to Manzanar. It was easy to get a job. I was already working there. They hired him, and we worked there until the camp was closed."[38]

After the closure of Manzanar, which included the removal of most of the buildings and structures, the site reverted gradually to its natural state. Beginning in 1969 annual pilgrimages have been sponsored by the Manzanar Committee, an activist group based in Los Angeles. Manzanar was designated a California Historical Landmark in 1972; it was added to the *National Register of Historic Places* in 1976; in 1985 it was designated a National Historic Landmark.

While the moral and constitutional issues have been debated for half a century, persons of Japanese ancestry have succeeded in securing some redress for their losses during World War II. On 10 August 1988, President Ronald Reagan signed the Civil Liberties Act of 1988, providing a restitution payment of twenty thousand dollars to each surviving internee. On 21 November 1989, President George H. Bush signed into law a measure establishing redress and an entitlement program. Accompanying the redress checks was a statement by President Bush: "A monetary sum and words alone cannot restore lost years or erase painful memories; neither can they fully convey our Nation's resolve to rectify injustice and to uphold the rights of individuals. We can never fully right the wrongs of the past. But we can take a clear stand for justice and recognize that serious injustices were done to Japanese Americans during World War II."[39]

On 3 March 1992, President Bush signed into law P.L. 102-248, an act of Congress establishing the Manzanar Historic Site, to be administered by the secretary of the interior as a unit of the National Park Service. Congress stated the purpose of the Manzanar Historic Site: "to provide for the protection and interpretation of the historical, cultural, and natural resources associated with the relocation of Japanese Americans during World War II."[40]

Viola's has this to say about the Manzanar Historic Site: "This was Native American land. . . . The Indians were definitely a part of that area, as well. I'm hoping it will be a monument not only to the early settlers [of Owens Valley] but also to the Indians that were here. The Japanese Americans are just as important. They were brought into a situation that certainly was not of their choosing. To a lesser degree and in a shorter period of time, what happened to them is what has been happening to the Native Americans."[41]

Viola at former WRA camp at Manzanar, June 1996.
Photo by the author.

7

Expanded Margins
Urban Opportunities

CONTRARY TO PREVALENT IMAGES IN POPULAR imagination, urbanization has long been a factor in the lives of the indigenous people of America. Stereotypes of "real" Indians, frozen in time in the last two decades of the nineteenth century and in place on the Great Plains, are deeply rooted in the American psyche. Michael Dorris, Modoc, has written: "Many non-Indians literally would not recognize a real Native American if they fell over one. . . . Learning about Native American culture and history is different from acquiring knowledge in other fields, for it requires an initial abrupt, and wrenching, demythologizing."[1] This demythologizing entails recognition that the majority of Indian people now live in cities. Regrettably, stereotypical images, reinforced by the media, persist.

Vi remembers that when she was teaching in the Los Angeles schools, Indian children would be teased, "If you're Indian, are you in the movies?"[2] When asked if she considers herself an urban Indian, Vi thought for a moment then responded,

"What other choices do I have?" After thinking about it for a few more minutes, she added, "Well, when you get right down to it, I guess I am. The majority of time I have lived in the city, and my experiences are mostly city experiences."[3] Viola has concentrated her commitment to the Los Angeles Indian community in two institutions, the American Indian Education Commission and the Native American Ministry of the Presbyterian Church. As a natural consequence of this significant involvement, she and her family have participated on a casual basis in pan-Indian activities such as powwows, most often as representatives of the education commission or the ministry.

American Indians have a long history in the Los Angeles basin, dating back to precontact times.[4] The most significant growth in American Indian population in Los Angeles occurred at the time that Viola and Andy Martinez moved to the city from Owens Valley. Andy typified the Indian veteran's experience. An estimated twenty-five thousand American Indians served in the U.S. armed forces during World War II. A higher percentage of Indians fought in World War II than any other ethnic group. Upon returning home, Indian veterans often found it difficult to fit into their native communities. Economic conditions on reservations meant few employment opportunities, and many returned veterans moved to cities in search of jobs.[5]

The population of Indians in Los Angeles quadrupled following World War II. The number of Indian veterans looking for work in the cities was magnified by the federally sponsored Termination and Relocation policy during the administration of President Dwight D. Eisenhower. The program was intended to terminate the federal government's responsibility for Indian interests and to relocate reservation Indians to the increasingly industrial areas of California and the Southwest. Ironically, the commissioner of Indian affairs at the time was Dillon S. Myer, former director of the War Relocation Authority from 1942 to 1946.[6]

As mentioned earlier, Tom Gustie was concerned that termination would be approved without people being fully aware of the consequences. He phoned Viola in Los Angeles, requesting that she come to the meeting in Bishop to explain the potential loss of benefits involved in approving termination. Some Owens Valley Paiutes were attracted to the idea of owning their property. Through her work with the Los Angeles welfare department, Vi had firsthand knowledge of people being denied essential services because they owned property. She remembers that while she was explaining these risks and the facts about taxation, the discussion became personal, with individuals reminding her that she owned a house in Los Angeles. She made clear that she did not yet own her home and that she would lose it if she could not pay the property taxes. Believing that many Owens Valley Paiutes were not well-informed about the risks, she asked who at the meeting was receiving indispensable aid, explaining to them, one by one, what their loss would be if termination were approved.

Owens Valley Paiutes were included in the Northern Paiute group during the termination era of the 1950s and early 1960s.[7] The Northern Paiutes were asked to draw up termination plans but ultimately refused to do so.[8] Viola believes she, together with others who opposed termination, including Tom Gustie, Samson Dewey, and Walter Bernard, provided a meaningful service to her people.[9]

Although Los Angeles was one of the target cities for relocation and job opportunities, Vi and Andy did not come to the city because of the Termination and Relocation program. They came because of job opportunities, as Vi recalls: "[Andy] wanted to find employment, and he wanted to come to Los Angeles for that. Naturally it was great for me, too, because I felt I could probably find a teaching job here [in Los Angeles]."[10] In a paper dated 21 June 1974, written for an education course, Viola stated, "These Indians from tribal, folk-centered cultures bring different values to the city. . . . Constant bills, lack of close friends, threat of lay-offs from jobs bother all but the most stable and competent. . . . If comparable job opportunities at home were available, it is probable that most of the Indians would remain on reservations."[11] Viola believes her statements are still valid today, more than twenty-five years later.

At the time that Vi and Andy moved to Los Angeles the postwar boom had made it extremely difficult to find housing. Vi remembers, "There was nothing [to rent]. Everybody was coming to Los Angeles."[12] Clara Moorhead, Viola's friend from Sherman Institute, had moved to the city several years before with her husband, Daniel Lopez. Andy and Daniel had also become friends at Sherman Institute. Clara and Danny invited Vi and Andy to live with them in an apartment in Venice, California, until a vacancy occurred in the same court.

Clara had started out in Los Angeles doing domestic work, for which she was trained at Sherman Institute, while her husband also found work commensurate with his training in semiskilled labor. Later, deviating from her boarding school training, Clara also found semiskilled employment. She recalls, "I worked in a place where they made those things that movie people sit on way up high. I also worked at a place where they made electrical equipment." When the war broke out, Clara went into aircraft manufacturing, becoming one of America's Rosie the Riveters:

> The reason I was a riveter was because I could fit into small places. I weighed a hundred pounds. We worked in a place right down here on Lincoln Boulevard. Whenever they needed help at one of the bigger places like Northrop, they would put us on a bus and take us out to help them.
>
> I liked it. I did a lot of other things besides riveting. I did punch-press. I did welding. They showed you and that was it. First time I used a punch-press, the guy showed me how to do it, and he said, "You've got to watch this arm up here. When it comes down, you've got to move." The first time I did it, it hit me right on the head.

I only had two boys that I worked [at riveting] with all the time. They were twins. I would do the shooting. We used to call it "bucking the ridge." They had a little bar—I was inside and they were on the outside. They wouldn't work with anybody else. It was really hard. You had to be real careful. If they missed the bucking part, it would throw me off rhythm, see. I wouldn't bawl them out [if they missed]. Anybody else they worked with would bawl them out. That's why they liked working with me.[13]

Andy Martinez found work as a carpenter, the job for which he was trained at Sherman Institute, but he was not sure he wanted to remain in the city. Because he was contemplating returning to Owens Valley, he discouraged Vi from committing to a teaching job in Los Angeles. Walter Heath, Viola's supervisor at Manzanar, was now an administrator in the Department of Charities in Los Angeles. Since she agreed with her husband that it would be difficult to leave a teaching job if they decided to return to Owens Valley, she applied for work with Heath. "Before going to Bishop, I had worked for the welfare department. It was a natural thing for me to see what I could get in the way of work through Mr. Heath. I went in one day and had a job the next day. Started right in."[14]

Viola's employment with the welfare department was similar to her previous social work. As a caseworker she had clients with varied needs, "whoever needed help. If I had not had an 'in' because of my previous employment and because of my knowing Mr. Heath, I'm sure I would have applied for a teaching job. I just felt it wasn't a bad idea to work as a social worker. I liked the work, I liked my clients."[15] She stayed in social work for approximately eight years until she and Andy, having chosen to remain in Los Angeles, decided to start a family.

When Vi found that she could not have children, she and Andy began looking into adoption. "Mr. Heath was also in charge of the adoption bureau. . . . So we went to him and talked about adoption."[16] Viola and Andy requested that the children they were to adopt be Paiute, and they have no reason to doubt that their request was honored.

Kirkland Robert, born 31 December 1952, was adopted in 1955 at age two. Vianne Lynn, born 25 December 1956, was adopted ten days later. When they were young and having birthday parties, to avoid conflicts with Christmas and New Year's Eve, they celebrated on days other than their actual birthdays. "We decided to pick days of our own, and their friends loved it. The kids understood these weren't their real birthdays. We celebrated their birthday *party* days."[17]

Kirk had been living in a foster home for the first two years of his life, and his foster parents told Vi and Andy that the boy had become very attached to an older man, a grandfather, in their family. They suggested that the transition to his new home would be eased if Vi and Andy could have someone in their home who would be like a grandpa. They invited Vi's Uncle Bob Somerville, who was in his late seventies, to stay with them. Vi says, "Elders are very important to Indians. He came down here and spent a month with us."

Vi is amused by a memory of Uncle Bob that contrasts urban and rural life:

> The thing that he noticed whenever we went anyplace was the fact that there were [uncultivated] fields and all they had in them were cars. He couldn't understand why. "What are all the cars doing there? Why is all this land taken up with cars?" Of course, we laughed about it. "They need a place to park the cars. You just can't leave them anyplace." Uncle Bob used an expression in Indian, *"Anaddibu!,"* meaning something like "Oh my goodness! You don't use the land to grow food? It's more important for your cars!" Every place we went, he was always saying, *"Anaddibu!* There's another one! Cars are more important!"[18]

Finally, "Grandpa" Bob said he had to go home to Owens Valley. Although they tried to make the parting as painless as possible, Kirk cried for two days. Vi and Andy promised to take

Kirk to visit "Grandpa." "When Bob did go back, we made a point of going up and visiting with him and being with him. Kirk preferred his company more than anyone's."[19]

Kirk remembers that, although Bob lived in a town called Basalt near the California-Nevada border, "I was pretty much at his side much of the time as a little one. I was really attracted to him. . . . We would just walk, just walk and talk."

Vianne's memories of Somerville are less intense but also affectionate. She was only four when he died, but somehow she has his "old wire-rimmed glasses," which she treasures. She remembers his cabinlike house. "He had all kinds of rocks all over the place. Pretty rocks that were cut with designs. Some of them were blue. Some were turquoise. Then quartz type rocks in different colors."[20]

Vi's memories of Uncle Bob explain, in part, his fascination with rocks:

> The family always talked about Uncle Bob. They called him the rich prospector because he liked to go out and really dig for whatever he could find.[21] That was his pastime. He always had money. Maybe there were times when he didn't have it, but when he did, he was always available to those in need.
>
> There is a road that goes from Bishop, up through Benton, on up to Hawthorne and on over to Reno. He covered that area, a great deal of it, because he was able to find mercury over there and gold and silver. He had a claim. I don't know how he did it. I just know he had a piece of land. He was probably told by someone that this is a good piece of land, you better hold on to it. And he did.
>
> While he had that, he was looking for other things. He ran across this line—the way he told me. He said he went into this dark place like a cave. He said he turned the flashlight on, and he thought he saw a line ahead of him, a little line in the ground. He said when he turned the flashlight off, he couldn't see it.
>
> He waited. When it was daylight enough, he went in and looked again. There was a blue line. I guess he knew about

turquoise. So he latched on to this land. He signed up for this spot. When he started to dig, he dug out turquoise. A lot of his turquoise was sold to Arizona—the Navajo people. He told me that himself. He said: "A lot of my turquoise they have down there in Arizona. I get rid of the turquoise when I need money."

These were things that I never paid too much attention to. It didn't mean that much to me. He was always trying to give me things, and I would say: "Uncle, you are not supposed to do that. That's yours. You don't just give it away." He said: "But I want you to have it." He gave me this [piece of turquoise]. I have just held on to it. When I was talking at a workshop at the Southwest Museum [in 1996] I showed the turquoise to the participants. This fellow said, "I know something about turquoise. Let me look at it." He had it for quite a while. When he brought it back, he said, "Don't you get rid of that. That's a pile of money." Wasn't that interesting?

Just before Uncle Bob died, he wanted to give things away. He wanted that taken care of. I didn't know it at the time, but he gave me this acreage in Nevada. I think because my sisters—they knew he was related, but I don't think they paid too much attention to him. I remembered that my aunt Mary Ann was very fond of him. When I went back up after my schooling, we had a chance to get together again. Naturally, he would come and visit my aunt, and she would go and visit him. When I was able to, I would go with her. We got reacquainted, my uncle and I. My husband and I spent a lot of time with him. When he died my husband and I were listed as his heirs. His wife and son had died. We were his only heirs.[22]

Both of Vi's children feel secure in their family. Kirk is not at all concerned about being adopted: "This has always been my family since I was a very young child. That's why I don't even think about being adopted. I don't like even talking about being adopted, because it doesn't have anything to do with my life."

Vianne says, "I think [my being adopted] is very positive. I mean, where would I be otherwise? I think whoever handled adoptions in the fifties did a great job. I thank God for that. . . . My parents are my parents. That's all I need to know." She has, however, wondered about the medical history of her birth parents. "Being a nurse and now that I have children, I would like to know some of the medical history. Am I going to have a cardiovascular disease or diabetes? Actually, I started wondering that when I became pregnant. My blood sugar went a little crazy. Native Americans have a really high potential for diabetes. . . . Then I have to go by faith. I have been healthy all my life. God has blessed me with health, and I am a strong person. [Adoption] is really not that important."

Despite living virtually their entire lives in the city, being educated in the Los Angeles school system, and having connections with the urban Indian community through their parents, their experiences in Owens Valley are of paramount importance to both Kirk and Vianne. Kirk remembers spending a lot of time in Owens Valley, beginning when he was four or five. He affectionately remembers Tom Gustie: "He couldn't see very well, but he would always go out and find his little fishing holes, which he would never tell anybody about, then come back with a load of fish." Vianne remembers "Grandpa Tom," as she alone called him, telling her stories about monsters that lived up in the mountains. "I liked him a lot, because he always seemed to like the kids."

Kirk's more recent memories include time spent with his uncle Harry Keller, the husband of Grace, who worked at Manzanar with Vi. Kirk and Harry, both avid fishermen, evidently are very companionable. "A lot of times we just travel around through the foothills or through the mountains. Just go up to different old mining camps. Just take trails and follow them and see where they take us. We talk about where they used to have the bootlegs and stuff like that in the old times. Where they had the liquor spots. Little mining towns, just the old trails they used to take in wagons going from Benton down to Bishop."

Vianne's memories, like Kirk's, are predominantly positive

regarding the visits to Owens Valley. "We went to fandangos, which are powwows. I remember seeing my relatives playing hand games." She vividly remembers pine-nutting with Minnie Williams: "My *mua* . . . she wasn't really my grandmother, but I called her *mua* because everyone called her *mua*. She was really good at pine-nutting. What I remember about her the most is when it was really cold, because we'd pine-nut in the fall, it would be frosty in the morning. She would get up really early and make sure we were all covered up. There would be frost on our bedrolls in the morning but we were warm because she would make sure we had enough blankets. She would always have a fire going first thing in the morning, with bacon cooking. Really good bacon, like homemade bacon. It would make you want to get out of bed."

Vianne reminisces about being taught how to harvest pine nuts by Minnie. "She was elderly but she was strong. We'd be huffing and puffing, but she wasn't. She'd carry a big stick and hit the trees. We'd have a tarp. We'd get the tarp down underneath the trees. We'd try to find a tree with the biggest pine nuts. Then she would save some and roast them in the ground so they were really good."

Kirk acknowledges that it is very important to him for people in the city to know that he is Indian: "When I meet them, in discussions, I let them know that I am American Indian." But he laughs and adds, "There is no grabbing them by the shirt and saying, 'I'm Indian.'" When asked if he remembers anything negative related to being Indian, he responds, "I don't think I have felt any negatives."

Vianne, however, relates negative experiences with Indians and non-Indians, both occurring in Owens Valley:

One time I was with one of my little cousins, and we were playing in the creek. They had a little waterhole where you could jump off this little bridge into the water. One of the girls kept pushing me into the water. I thought she was playing at first, then I realized she was being malicious. She didn't know that I am a really good swimmer because I used to swim in the ocean. I finally got mad at her and pushed her underneath the water. I think I was about twelve at the time and I was pretty strong. Even though I was skinny, I was pretty strong because I swam a lot.

I remember holding her underneath the water for quite a while. All of a sudden bubbles started coming up. Then I realized I'd better let go of her, because she might drown. After that she never bothered me anymore. I think she thought I didn't belong there because I was from L.A., and I'm fair [complexioned], and they probably thought I was not Indian.

When Vianne relates the following experience, she does so with residual distress: "In Bishop they didn't know I was from the reservation part of town, and I could hear white people talk about my relatives—that they are drunken, lazy. It made me really angry. At first, I felt like I had to defend them, and then I gave up this idea because I knew it wouldn't change things."

Scholarship in twentieth-century Indian history has often assumed that Indian urbanization is a by-product of the federal government's injudicious Termination and Relocation program, which been destructive to Indian people.[23] Kirk and Vianne's assertions contradict this assumption.

Kirk is strongly influenced by his mother's "coming off the reservation and making something of herself." He believes that Indian people should, like his parents, "get off the reservation. I think that is holding them back. They don't necessarily need to move to a city, but they have to move off the reservation." He modifies this opinion: "I can't speak for the whole group. Some of the reservation Indians do fine for themselves. There are others that don't."

Although Vianne admires her father for working hard and being creative, she credits her mother with pushing her to get an education. "I'm really grateful that I did, because [otherwise] I wouldn't have been able to be a nurse. It takes a lot of education to become a nurse." Vianne says that her brother is also a role model. "We are very, very close. We can tell what the other is thinking just by looking at each other. We stick up for each other. We always have."

Like her brother, Vianne says it is very important to her that people in the city know she is Indian:

So I tell people. Because I don't look Indian, I figure the only way they will know is if I tell them. . . . Like one lady at work, when I said I'm part Indian, she goes, "I thought they died or something." She thought they have nothing to do with today's society. [Sometimes] because of my looks they say, "Yeah, you're a wanna-be." I say, "You are just stereotyping. You think I'm supposed to have black hair." If you are 100 percent, your genial type will show that you are Indian. But if you are mixed, it might not. I look at it scientifically sometimes.

I think you should be proud of what you are. I think the self-esteem of Indian kids needs to be raised. Education needs to be pushed. It's hard to do that when there are no role models and no drive. . . . I think part of it is the isolation [on the reservation]. There is just so much more here in the city that we see as role models. There's the media, there're the schools, there are all kinds of cultural influences, more of everything. When you are isolated away from all that, and you have a lot of poverty . . . well, poverty is not a culture. I think people think Indians like to live that way. You know, just because they are poor doesn't mean it's part of their culture.

Vi and Andy were divorced in 1973.

I did say to Andy, "We are fortunate we have our children. We have been very, very lucky. I would like us to stay a family in that respect. . . . I'm sure there are a lot of things you don't like about me, and there are a lot of things I don't like about you. But there are a lot of things I love about you, and I hope that there are things that you love about me. I would just as soon, if it is humanly possible, that no words go out of my mouth that discredit you and cause our children to think less of you as a father.[24]

Kirk and Vianne maintain good relations with both parents. Kirk has a close relationship with Andy, which includes frequent contact. With his mother he has a close and protective bond. Vianne reflects on the divorce: "I think it was probably the right thing to do because my mom has a good life on her own. She is productive and happy. My dad also has a good life. They don't live under the same roof anymore, so it could make it difficult for holidays, but we have always managed ways to work that out. My parents were together for a very long time, and there are a lot of friends that they actually grew up with, as well as relatives they grew up with. I have gone to Sherman Institute reunions with both of them."

Wedding of Vianne and Kirk Wentzell, 1 May 1993, at St. John's Presbyterian Church, Los Angeles. Left to right: Vianne's father Andy, brother Kirk, Vianne, bridegroom Kirk, mother Viola.

A major aspect in Kirk's and Vianne's ties to their mother is their early involvement in the Presbyterian Church. Vi believes that her exposure on the reservation to Presbyterian missionaries resulted in a natural inclination toward this church. She credits Kirk, however, for her engaging in regular attendance at services. "He was the one that came to me and said he wanted to go to church. I remember I teased him and asked, 'Why do you want to go to church?' He said: '[The neighbors] get dressed up every Sunday, and they go to church, and they have fun.'"

Since Andy, a nonpracticing Catholic, had no objection, Viola and Kirk and later Vianne began attending a Presbyterian church. "Kirk wanted to be baptized, so we three were baptized. Since I had decided that I would not seek a teaching position until they were old enough to be on their own, but I wanted to keep my hand in teaching a little, I volunteered to teach Sunday school. And so I learned a great deal. I learned a lot about my faith. It was a natural thing for me to do. As a result, during the summer months I decided that I wanted to be involved with the summer youth program." Under the auspices of this program church members and their children traveled to various areas to renovate or enlarge churches that were in need of help.

> Each year, as my children grew up, I continued to be involved. At Las Vegas, New Mexico, the people themselves arranged through the Presbyterian Church for us to come and do some renovation work. . . . Then we went to Tuba City, Arizona, where we actually added on a classroom. . . . While all of this was going on, I was the only Indian at our church. I began to think: There are Presbyterian Churches on a lot of the reservations. A lot of Indian people come to Los Angeles. Why aren't they coming to church? I asked the minister why we weren't going out and helping Indians to come to our church. Why is it we are sending money out of the country to groups to persuade them to become Presbyterian, and we've got people here in the city that have been exposed to the Presbyterian Church, and there's no place for them? Then somehow the church members talked about it.[25]

From these discussions in the original five-person committee, including Vi, emerged a resolve to form a Native American Ministry in Southern California. Having established relationships with the principal individuals and agencies in the Los Angeles County Indian community, Vi describes how the committee endeavored to collect the essential demographic data:

> We had a survey, which was difficult because we have no Indian ghetto. We hired Roxanne Burgess, a Yurok from northern California who was Presbyterian and was working with the Southern California Indian Center. We found out that there were certainly enough Presbyterians here,[26] but they were not in a situation to set up a church just for themselves. . . . Because of the locations of Indians in the various areas, it was decided that the thing to do was to see if we could have four churches that would let their facilities be used in the afternoon. So that is what we have been doing. It finally worked out that we have services every other Sunday in four different areas—Pasadena, Westchester, Long Beach, and Tustin.

These services are held in the afternoon so as to avoid conflict with morning services in other churches. "The people themselves have a part in the service. They are connected. There is a storytelling time, a time to entertain by sharing your skills, your art, your musical talents. Then afterwards a potluck. It always ends with a potluck. To Indians it's strange when you get through with a get-together and you just leave. You are supposed to be family. How can you be family if you don't sit and eat together?"

Vi persuaded Andy's cousin, Sheila Gustie Martinez, to become involved in the Native American Ministry. Sheila describes her participation:

> In Bishop I always participated in going to church. Here [in Pasadena] I got more involved with the church when I got involved with the Native American Ministry project. Vi Martinez had spoken to me a few times about it. I started

going to the other areas. I just got interested in meeting more people. Everyone was so friendly. Of course, Vi said, "You don't have to worry, we always eat. There is always a pot-luck." I guess that's what got me going, too. Then they started having a worship service in Pasadena at the Conwood Pres-byterian Church on Rosemead and California [Boulevards]. We meet second and fourth Sundays.

I got interested in the people. Most of them have lived here, maybe, all their lives. Native American and they don't know what a reservation is like. I feel bad because they have no reservation, a lot of them. The Native American Ministry fills a need for these people.

I am on the steering committee. We meet once a month and discuss the ministry and what things should be done. We have to plan for the worship every month. We have to make sure we contact who is going to do the main meat dish for the meetings. All the offerings taken at worship go to a burial fund. Our minister lets us know who he helped for the month. It doesn't have to be anybody involved with the Ministry, it's any Native American. Like if they need a hundred dollars for transportation to get home if somebody dies. For people who pass away here, we help with the funeral expenses. That's where our money goes that's taken up for worship. We also have an emergency fund that helps some people that may need electricity or something like that.

The Ministry meets at 2:30 in the afternoon. They chose that time so you can go to your own church worship service. You could be Catholic and go to your own service, then go to fellowship at the Ministry service.

To get on the steering committee, they just ask whoever in the congregation might be interested. You only stay [on the committee] two years, then somebody will suggest a good candidate. I got a call from our minister out of the clear one night. That just surprised me. He asked if I would be inter-ested and I said, "Yes, I'll try it."

To raise funds we have dinners, like fry bread meals. We all work together. There are certain people that do good fry bread, so they are always asked. It's more of the extended family idea, just an automatic thing.

First of all, I started going to worship just out of something to do and mainly to meet more people. I have enjoyed it. The involvement with the Ministry made me closer to and more aware of God. More so than a regular church service. I was just more comfortable. I've gone to several Presbyterian churches here that are huge. Something like that is too overwhelming. The Ministry is more intimate, more family like. It's very small, but we want it to grow. I guess some Native Americans think you have to be Presbyterian to go [to Ministry services]. But it's not true. That's why we're trying to reach out to people. We are trying to reach people, especially, who are into their traditional ways because we know it's good to do both.

I think it's getting better. We just say, "Please join us." Potlucks always, I think, get a lot of people. We are just a big family. That makes them relax so they enjoy it. It's needed in the city very much. A lot of work needs to be done for the respect of Native American people. A lot of work has to be started with the youth, because the youth have been left out. I think they've been told they can't get anywhere. We [in the Ministry] are trying because we have a big youth conference with the Presbyterian Church. There are also activities going on here [in the city] for youth. A lot of Native American people are involved with that.

Native Americans, from what I see, are very quiet people. Once they get with a group, like a powwow, everybody is laughing and happy because there are a lot of Native Americans there. So a ministry is needed, because once they are there, they can relax, talk to each other, get acquainted. Then they find out they have more friends.

As I said, Native Americans, the majority of them, are very quiet people. That's something that is inbred. It's nothing you wanted to be, but you are just quiet. Once you get acquainted with others, you come out of your shell, and it's more relaxing. You get to know that there are other people going through something similar as you are. I guess that's how I got involved, because of my problems, and it brought me closer to God. Now that I don't have the responsibility anymore of raising a family, it gives me more time to work for God. It gives me a lot of comfort, working with the Ministry and for God. It just made everything balanced.

I plan to move back to Bishop because it's my home. If I could be of any help here [in the city] I'd come back and forth and do whatever I can. Because I've made a lot of friends now, from all tribes, with the Ministry, if I could be of any help, sure, I'd be back.[27]

Viola articulates the elements in the Christian religion that coincide with the traditional beliefs of her Paiute family: "The idea of loving one another, of being helpful, taking care of one another. I remember my Uncle Bob saying, 'We don't have to have insurance policies. We take care of one another.' Those were things I would think about when I would compare the words in the Bible to the things my uncles had taught me. The Paiutes had a deep faith."[28]

8

Education Advocate
Eighteen Years in the Los
Angeles Unified School District

During Kirk's and Vianne's formative years
Viola was an at-home mom, while Andy's carpentry work developed into his own contracting business. Among other volunteer work, Vi was active in
the Parent Teacher Association, serving as president
at Walgrove Elementary School. "Imagine!" she has
said to me several times, "An Indian president of
the PTA!" She also served as treasurer at Mark
Twain Junior High school. It was not until 1968,
when Kirk was almost sixteen and Vianne was
twelve, that Vi began her teaching career, twenty-
nine years after earning her teaching credential at
Santa Barbara State College.

> I started teaching at 116th Street School. My first
> class was fifth grade, and then I asked to go
> down to the fourth grade. It was awfully hard. It
> was very difficult. They were just not at grade
> level. After eight years in the inner city, I trans-
> ferred to Mar Vista.

It was a long drive to 116th Street. I learned from some of the other teachers that if you had a good enough reason, you could request a transfer to a school closer to your home. I did. It was ignored. In the meantime I had become a part of the American Indian Education Commission. Joanne Morris, who was the first director of the commission, went to the [school] board. She informed them that I had requested reassignment and wondered why it was not pursued. Shortly afterward, I got a call asking me if I would be interested in teaching at Mar Vista Elementary School. I had never heard of Mar Vista Elementary School, so I said, "I don't think so. Let me think about it."

When I came home, I said, "Where is Mar Vista? My kids said: "Mar Vista is real close, Mom. Why don't you take Mar Vista?" I said, "I don't know where it is." They said, "It's right over the hill." We drove over there. There it was, nine-tenths of a mile. I called them back and said yes! That's how I got to Mar Vista.

[At Mar Vista] they asked me to teach the upper grades. When I started to teach sixth grade, I found, again, that the some of the children were not at grade level. I found myself working with two sets of lesson plans. I was working at grade level to not shortchange my students who were at grade level. I also had to really work at a lower level to get those students up to grade. We ranged from thirty-two to thirty-six students and we had no aides. I then decided that I would prefer working with younger children. I remembered how difficult it had been for me when I was learning English in Benton and how I felt when I finally could read and write. I decided that maybe I should start teaching third grade.

That summer I went down to the Board of Education office and told them what I wanted to do. They wanted to know why. I told them, "I know the problems I had as an Indian. I couldn't speak a word of English [when I started to school]." [I told them] how it was having to learn English and how good I felt when I was able to speak English. I felt that if I could work with students at a younger age and explain to them how important it was to speak really good

English and to study hard so they could read and write well, it would make a big difference. Because it sure did with me. I convinced them to let me teach third grade conditionally while I worked on my elementary credential.

I went to summer school, and I took classes during the school year for about two years at UCLA. I got my elementary credential, and I stayed at the third-grade level the rest of the time until I retired in 1984. The minute that I started to teach the third grade with a population of whites, Mexicans, and Orientals, my thought was "We are a mixed family."

I remember I introduced myself as Mrs. Martinez, and I asked them, "What does it make you think when you hear Mrs. Martinez?" A hand went up. "You're Spanish." I said, "Think again." "Mexican." "Think again." They couldn't. I said, "Look around you." I had Indian baskets, I had pottery around, [but] no one ever guessed I was Indian. I said, "I brought them because I am American Indian." "Oh!" That started us.

Then I said: "Friday is going to be food day. This Friday we are going to have some Indian food." I brought in fry bread. They thought it was just great. I told them, "On Fridays we will take a different student and you will bring in something that your family eats a lot of."

And then we would talk about the food and the culture, and we would write about it. We would do spelling words about it. We'd use measurements for arithmetic. Chemistry was our water, our milk, and things of that sort. And we learned about one another. I told them things about myself and the way I grew up and how I had to learn, how difficult it was, and how people made fun of me for the way I talked. As we learned about one another, we found something that we liked about one another. One of the best class get-togethers was when two Japanese mothers asked if they could prepare a Japanese meal and have all of the parents come in. I said, "You bet! Do you also have a dance you could do?" [One mother] said, "You bet!" By Christmas time, we were a definite family. I never had discipline problems.[1]

Viola during her teaching career, date unknown
(probably early 1980s). She is wearing a beaded
Paiute medallion that she handcrafted.

Vi retired from teaching in 1984. In a paper for a class at UCLA, dated 19 March 1990, Vianne wrote about her mother's final day of her teaching career.

> The school planned a whole day in her honor, which was very unusual; this had never been done for a teacher at this school before. All the children brought flowers and wore her favorite color—lavender. There was an assembly out on the play yard. The children sang a song they composed for her and gave her a scrapbook with many pictures. Her family and many of her friends were present. A few of her former students who were already in college were there. . . . They remember her as the first teacher who told them that Christopher Columbus did not discover America. Indian people were already here, so how could he have discovered it?[2]

Viola's teaching career led to her being a founding member of the American Indian Education Commission (AIEC) of the Los Angeles Unified School District (LAUSD). She describes the origin and history of the commission.[3] It began with a meeting in Los Angeles of the Indian Education Association, a national organization. At this meeting Vi met Sanford Smith, a Ute Indian and an attorney who became active in LAUSD affairs. She and Smith developed the idea to start a local Indian education group. "Somehow Sanford got other Indians involved, and we started to have meetings. Then Sanford Smith and some of the black teachers thought, 'Maybe we ought to get together and let the Board of Education know that we need representation with the Board, that we need to be able to speak directly to them.' Who could we interact with who would be concerned in knowing how the children were getting along in the urban setting?"

As a result, they decided to form commissions for the ethnic groups that were represented in Los Angeles schools. Vi remembers that the original AIEC in 1976 had about twenty or thirty charter members. "We were teachers who were concerned. We had parents of children in school who were concerned. My feeling was at the time that we needed to make sure that the people who started [the commission] were the parents and teachers of the children who were definitely involved. And we did."

From the beginning one of the AIEC's priorities was to educate non-Indians about Indian people. "I'm not saying the education system is wrong," says Viola. "It isn't wrong. We need to be educated, but we are not an oddity. . . . We are people. I would like to know what [non-Indians] have in mind. Are they thinking of me as an ignorant person without any capabilities or are they thinking that maybe there is something here which is interesting, meaningful, and worth finding out about?" Vi expresses great concern that too many young Indian people feel that they do not have much to offer "because they are constantly questioned. They are constantly made to feel that no one really knows much about them. 'The Indian' doesn't exist in the way that non-Indians assume."

When Viola learned of my work refuting stereotypes of Indian people, she invited me to apply for membership on the commission. My two years of service on the AIEC, from 1996 to 1998, were exceptionally rewarding. I acquired valuable insights regarding urban Indians and was given opportunities to contribute in many ways to the Los Angeles Indian community. Above all, after serving on the commission with Viola, I have profound admiration for her dedication and hard work on behalf of Indian children.

John Orendorff, a member of the Western Band of the Cherokee Nation and director of the AIEC during its final years, expresses Vi's contribution to the commission: "I think Viola's greatest contribution was being a California Indian elder who kept us on track. Often the plight of the California Indian is ignored. The Native peoples of California are underrepresented in arts and education, partially because of the perception by non-Indians that other Indian cultures are more glamorous. Viola kept us on track [by reminding us] that the commission was created for California children, specifically for the educa-

tion of the children in Los Angeles. She really had that as her
mandate, to keep us from getting distracted and forgetting what
was important."

After more than twenty years of service to the nation's most
populous urban Indian community, the Los Angeles AIEC was
forced to disband permanently on 30 June 1998, a victim of

Viola receiving an award for her work with the
LAUSD American Indian Education Commis-
sion. Presenting the award is John Orendorff,
Cherokee, director of the commission.
Photo courtesy of John Orendorff.

California's Proposition 209, which was intended to eliminate racial and gender preferences in public agencies. Although the termination of the ethnic commissions occurred abruptly, deliberations had taken place over several months, as the Board of Education privately evaluated its compliance with Proposition 209, which was approved by voters in 1996 but was not implemented until it was upheld by the courts in the fall of 1997. The board of the LAUSD, the nation's second largest, voted on 13 April 1998 to replace the AIEC and six other education commissions with a single Human Relations Commission, citing the necessity of accommodating the post–Proposition 209 environment.

"The greatest loss to the Indian community in Los Angeles," says Viola, "is educational advocacy for our children. What will happen to our young people in this urban setting?"

This advocacy has, however, sometimes generated controversy. The AIEC cause that generated the most heated controversy and media attention during the commission's tenure was the successful crusade to abolish the adoption of Indian names and images as Los Angeles school mascots. After years of struggle, this feat was finally accomplished in 1997 by twenty-nine volunteers and the AIEC's director, John Orendorff.

Orendorff denies that the AIEC was in conflict with either the intent or the letter of Proposition 209. "That [charge] really hurt me. I very strongly disagreed with the district's stand that we were a liability under [Proposition] 209. We were not an exclusive organization. We took advice from and gave advice to all. I would say that 60 percent of my work was done with the non-Indian community. The state mandates curriculum which includes American Indian studies, especially in the elementary grades.... We assisted with that.... We [commissioners] would never discriminate against anybody.... We were open to all."

By the time of the AIEC's termination, Viola had held every office, including chair, vice-chair, secretary, and treasurer and was then serving as chair of the finance committee. She and the other volunteers worked to fulfill the mandates of the AIEC, which included assisting Indian parents and students with school issues, supporting Indian teachers in personnel matters, educating non-Indian personnel about Indian culture and values and about how best to work with Indian students, and advising the LAUSD on policy issues relating to American Indians.

Orendorff asks: "Who will now fulfill these mandates? We [Indians] are less than 1 percent in the District. There are still fifteen hundred youngsters who need representation. . . . My fear is that it will go back to the way it always was [before the AIEC] and other people will have to speak for us. We will have to rely on a non-Indian educator to understand our issues, speak to our issues, to even bring forward our issues."

Like Orendorff, Viola has little confidence that the LAUSD's Human Relations Commission will be able to carry out these mandates. "How can they? They don't understand the problems of Indians. Because they don't have enough information regarding Indian issues, these issues get tabled 'for further study.'" When asked who will now speak for Indian children in Los Angeles, Vi says: "That's what I want to know. We may never see another Indian present at a school board meeting. The abolishment of the commission is another episode in a long history of broken treaties."

Orendorff insists: "We are resilient and we will not go away. We can suffer tremendous setbacks and never give up." Viola agrees that Indian people are "not going to disappear." Further, she argues: "Efforts by Indian people to take care of themselves, independent of government agencies, will ultimately be stronger endeavors."

Detail from photo on page 148.

9

The Trip Home

FROM 20 JUNE TO 24 JUNE 1996, VIOLA AND I AND
Barbara Arvi, director of education for the Southwest Museum in Los Angeles, toured Owens Valley
by car.[1] The trip was very emotional for Vi, who
frequently expressed gratitude for being able to
recapture her earlier life in a way she had never
done before.

20 June

We three drove from Los Angeles to the town
of Mammoth Lakes in two cars, Vi riding with
Barbara since they had not been together in several
months. After lunch in Mojave, we drove north on
Highway 395, originally called El Camino Sierra.
Funds for the construction of the paved highways,
260 miles between Mojave and Bridgeport, were
appropriated in California's first bond issue in 1910.
The first 10-mile segment was completed in 1916,
and finally in 1931 there were paved highways the
entire distance between Los Angeles and Bishop.
The four-lane portion of 395 on which we traveled,
from Sherwin Summit to Highway 203 leading to

CHAPTER

Mammoth Lakes, was completed in 1956. On this entire drive we had uninterrupted views of two dramatic, snow-crested mountain ranges, the Sierra Nevada to the west and the White-Inyo to the east, towering thousands of feet above.

We stopped in Independence, a town that had been closely linked to mines in the Sierra Nevada and Inyo Mountains. Due to a significant combination of mining and agriculture the town assumed a leading role in civic affairs until the late nine-

Viola Martinez and Barbara Arvi on the trip home, June 1996.
Photo by the author.

teenth century.[2] Our purpose in stopping there was to visit the Eastern California Museum, which archives artifacts and materials on the natural history, indigenous people, early settlers, and contemporary history of the Eastern Sierra. One of its most valuable resources is the documentation of the Manzanar War Relocation Authority camp.

Vi, who had never before been in the museum, was drawn as if by a magnet to a display of photographs at the rear of the room. She immediately located a picture identified as her mother, Ivy Lent Meroney, holding "baby boy." Viola and I were astonished by this discovery. Vi, however, pointed out to Kathy Barnes, the museum's curator, that the baby could not be a boy because it was resting in a girl's cradleboard. The sunshades on boys' cradleboards were decorated with diagonal lines, whereas those for girls had zigzag lines or diamonds. The curator immediately recognized the error and asked Vi to identify the baby, but, since the photo was undated, she could not. Another photo of a mother nursing her baby with the caption "Meals at all hours" is identified as "Ivy Lent Powers Meroney Torres [with] baby Edith Powers." Both photos were taken by A. A. Forbes, who toured Owens Valley around the turn of the century, taking Madonna-like pictures of Paiute women with their babies as well as of scenery and other aspects of Owens Valley life.

There was a photo, also taken by Forbes and dated 1912, that was identified as Edna Tom. The baby she is holding is not identified but is most likely her daughter Hazel. Edna is Vi's sister, the second oldest child of Ivy Lent Meroney.

Curator Kathy Barnes, who was extremely well informed and helpful, asked Vi where she grew up, and upon learning that it was in Benton, told us that the museum had a collection of photos taken by Burton Frasher at Benton. She promised to take them out of storage for us to peruse later on our way back home.

Leaving Independence, we continued through Big Pine, beneath the Pacific Crest Trail, which rises to nearly fourteen

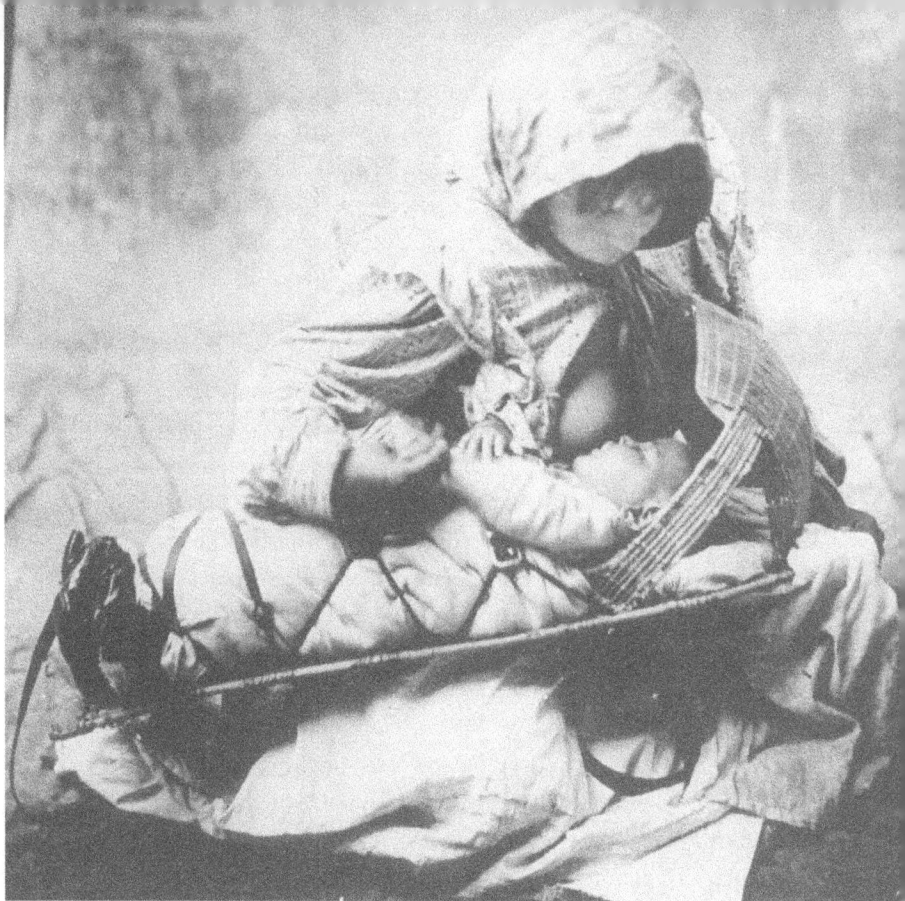

Viola's mother, Ivy Lent Meroney, with
baby tentatively identified as Edith.
Photo by A. A. Forbes. Courtesy of Eastern California Museum.

thousand feet; through Bishop, home to the Owens Valley
Paiute-Shoshone Indian Cultural Center; and then we headed
west on Highway 203 to Mammoth Lakes, where Barbara had
invited us to stay at her restful and attractive condominium.
Contrary to expectation, Mammoth Lakes is not named after
the impressive mountains that surround it; rather, its name
comes from a mine called Mammoth, located in Mono County
in 1877. Although the Mammoth mine bonanza never materi-
alized, the brief gold rush created roads important to later

settlers. A different kind of bonanza developed later when tourists discovered the natural attractions of the Eastern Sierra. Year-round recreation is Mono County's primary source of income, generating eight to ten times the value of mining, ranching, and lumbering combined. "Lakes" was added to the name by the post office to avoid confusion with another town in California named Mammoth.

Later that evening at Barbara's condo Vi and I were alone while Barbara was shopping for groceries. Vi became very emotional, wondering why she had not known about the photos at the Eastern California Museum. I tried to assure her that the photographer, A. A. Forbes, had almost certainly never given copies of the photos to her family, that photographers routinely appropriated images of Native people at the turn of the century. She seemed to feel better after hearing this.

21 June

Viola, Barbara, and I visited for two hours with Nancy Peterson Walter at her home in Mammoth Lakes. Nancy Walter had written her doctoral dissertation on the Land Exchange Act of 1937, which created the reservations at Bishop, Big Pine, and Lone Pine. Previously she had told me that she had pictures of Vi's family of which, she was confident, Vi was not aware. Kathy Barnes had told us that Nancy Walter had done considerable work on the Forbes collection, which was archived by the Natural History Museum of Los Angeles.

Nancy produced several albums of the Forbes pictures. She has spent over twenty years identifying the subjects of the photographs, primarily relying on the help of Paiute elders. When she showed us the one of Edna Tom that we had seen in the Eastern California Museum, we questioned the 1912 date. Nancy agreed that the date could be inaccurate but believed the photo could not have been taken much later than 1913. She produced a document from the Los Angeles Department of Water and Power, a kind of census of Paiutes in the areas

Viola's mother, Ivy Lent Meroney, with baby. Note the zigzag lines on the cradleboard, indicating that the baby is a girl.

Photo by A. A. Forbes. Courtesy of Eastern California Museum.

where the utility wanted to obtain water rights. Vi, who was at Sherman Institute at the time, was listed as being eighteen years old in 1930, whereas she most likely was twelve. I questioned the source of the information for the survey, and Nancy assured me it was quite accurate, "more accurate than the records of the Bureau of Indian Affairs." I continued to question the sources, however, and Nancy admitted that someone in the community had to have listed Vi as being eighteen, possibly without really knowing.

Vi asked who the elders were who identified her family's photos, then objected that at least some of these elders did not know her family. Vi and I later came to the same conclusion about the Forbes collection—that some of the individuals in the photographs may have been misidentified. We were reminded of the complexity and difficulty inherent in the kind of ethnographic work in which Nancy Walter was engaged.

In the afternoon we drove Highway 120 west to Tioga Pass—at 9,945 feet, the highest highway pass in California. This was a journey to which Vi did not relate at all. She had taken trips with Aunt Mary Ann over the pass but on a different route. She said that she felt sad and out-of-place. Nothing was familiar.

Her spirits rose, however, as we returned to Highway 395 and headed toward the little town of Lee Vining, named after Leroy Vining, reputed to be the first prospector in the Mono Basin. On the east side of town we visited the Schoolhouse Museum, with a beautiful view of Mono Lake and the Mono Craters. The old Mono Lake schoolhouse, originally located by DeChambeau Creek, five miles north of Lee Vining, was moved to its present location in 1988 and converted into a museum.[3]

Here at the Schoolhouse Museum were housed the artifacts of the Mono Basin Historical Society, including historic photographs. Vi discovered a picture of Carrie Bethel, a cousin of Aunt Mary Ann. There were also photos of the Keller family, including Lester Keller, who was George Washington's son-in-law and the father of Harry Keller, whom we would meet the following day. Harry Keller's mother Mabel is Vi's first cousin, her father being Ivy Lent Meroney's brother. I was beginning to realize that Vi's family in the Owens Valley was extended indeed, in "the Indian way," as Vi says.

22 June

Eleanor Bethel, Vi's cousin and Carrie Bethel's neice-in-law, met us at Barbara's condo. Eleanor, nicknamed Blondie, is the sister of Evelyn (Fuzzy), with whom Vi climbed into the palm trees at Sherman Institute to speak Paiute. Her father is Louis Williams, Mary Ann's nephew, and her mother is Minnie Williams. Eleanor is called Big Auntie by Kirk and Vianne. Viola, Barbara, Eleanor, and I spent this day touring the length and breadth of Owens Valley, including the backcountry, with Eleanor pointing out noteworthy features, such as pine-nutting sites.

Our first stop, about three miles east of Highway 395 on a gravel road, was the hot springs of Hot Creek geologic site, where hot springs, warm springs, and *famaroles* (gas vents) abound.[4] Eleanor walked around the area for a few minutes and came back to the car with what appeared to us to be a precontact obsidian scraper. We all took this discovery—appropriately, as it turned out—as a portent of a rewarding day.

Eleanor introduced Barbara and me to the specifics of the *piüga* caterpillar eaten by traditional Paiutes. These caterpillars, larvae of the Pandora moth, live in Jeffrey pines and were harvested into steep-sided trenches surrounding the trees. A single camp of Paiutes could gather a ton or more, which were cooked in a fire pit with hot coals, then dried. They were eaten either in this simple form or were mixed with pine nuts and sunflower seeds.[5]

We drove the June Lake Loop, which branches off Highway 395 to the June Lake basin (abounding with campgrounds, resorts, stores, and boat landings) and reconnects with the highway north of Grant Lake. The loop offers wide, sandy

Viola's sister Edna Tom, with baby, possibly Edna's daughter Hazel.
Photo by A. A. Forbes in 1912. Courtesy of Eastern California Museum.

beaches; views of Carson Peak, rising 10,909 feet above June Lake; and Reversed Peak, so named because of a creek originating in June Lake and flowing toward rather than away from the mountains. The road follows the shore of the lake through the community of June Lake, then past Gull Lake, named for the gulls that frequent the area looking for fish after flying from their nesting area on Mono Lake. As we drove through these various scenic areas, with the wild roses and irises in bloom, Viola exclaimed, "I *walked* this as a child!"

Later we explored the site of the abandoned Mono Mills, a sizable sawmill that had supplied Bodie mining enterprises with wood for domestic use and for fueling the steam engines and hoisting works from 1878 to 1916.[6] As we were walking around the site, Vi said to Eleanor, "Can't you imagine Aunt Mary Ann walking with us, saying, 'There is more I could tell you.'"

At the Keller family cemetery, Eleanor recalled that Mabel Keller had felt uncomfortable climbing the rocks around the cemetery. Whenever she did, the wind came up as though she were being told to leave. As we were standing in the cemetery, Viola made a formal assertion: "This cemetery says that we [Indians] are a part of the white world now, while we are still retaining our land and our ways. The Christian crosses on the graves show that we have accepted the way things are now."

Later as we drove home through the valley, Viola said that Aunt Mary Ann used to tell her, "A long time ago all this land belonged to us, and we could leave our baskets and other things as long as we wanted and return to find them undisturbed."

23 June

There was much emotion on this day! Barbara, Vi, and I visited Harry Keller and his Nez Perce wife, Grace, who is called Little Auntie by Kirk and Vianne. The Keller home was located near Benton, which is situated in high country, at an elevation of six thousand feet. This village, where Vi spent her early years with Aunt Mary Ann, was once a riotous mining town, thriving from

1864 to 1881 in the Blind Springs Mining District, from which was extracted four million dollars in silver. There is speculation that the town may have been named after John C. Frémont's father-in-law, Senator T. H. Benton of Missouri, who was a proponent of gold and silver currency.

Harry and Grace greeted us warmly. Harry was charmingly talkative. He began by showing us intricate and beautiful bead-work done by his mother, a celebrated beadworker whose

Viola with her cousin Harry Keller and his wife, Grace, who worked with Vi at Manzanar.
Photo by the author.

Highly valued beadwork by Mabel Keller,
the mother of Harry, Viola's cousin.
Photo by the author.

creations are coveted by collectors and museums. Grace also
showed us old baskets, including the last one made by Aunt
Mary Ann. I respectfully asked if I could take a photo of that
basket, and Grace generously assured me I could take any
photos I wanted and displayed the baskets and beadwork so I
could photograph them.

We visited the little cemetery at Benton, where the George
Washington clan is buried. There they were—the names Vi had
mentioned in her narrative, including Aunt Mary Ann.

As we drove with Harry and Grace into the center of Benton,
Vi related a memorable incident from her childhood. Vi and a
friend, Ada Salque, were walking home from school and found
cigarettes. They went inside a barn belonging to the Bramlett
family, sat on a bale of hay, and smoked. Feeling dizzy, they
stomped out the remainder of the stubs in the barn. The barn
did not catch fire, but embers burned pinpoint holes in Vi's
clothes. Aunt Mary Ann detected the holes and the smell of
cigarette smoke on Vi's clothes. Vi says she was so astonished at

her aunt's accusation—"You have been smoking!"—that Vi thought her aunt must have been a witch.

As we drove down a steep incline and rounded a curve, there lay the village of Benton in a small valley framed by the snow-covered Sierra. Near the old trading post, now abandoned, is a relatively new tourist shop. The tourist shop and surrounding property are owned by the Bramlett family, who most likely purchased them from a man named Davis, the rancher who charged George Washington's family one dollar a year to live on the land. The Bramletts owned the property in Benton when Vi was living there with her aunt.

The Bramletts had refused Grace permission for us to walk to the hot springs and the dilapidated and abandoned houses where Viola had lived as a child. Vi left us all at the tourist shop and went to talk to the Bramlett matriarch. When she returned to us, she reported that she had obtained permission, then she bent over, sobbing: "I'm home!"

Mrs. Bramlett was concerned about our injuring ourselves in the exceedingly hot water of the springs, and she also worried about our starting a fire in the dry brush surrounding the springs. She asked Vi if she smoked, and Vi answered, "I haven't touched a cigarette since I was a kid and almost set your barn on fire." This evidently broke the ice, then Vi told Mrs. Bramlett that she had brought along two white friends to whom she had to prove that she was an Indian! Grace was astonished that Vi had obtained permission but explained to me that she, herself, is persona non grata with the Bramlett family. "That old trading post is full of Paiute artifacts that belong to the Washington clan and I told her so."

As we walked to the hot springs, I was in a state of high anticipation. The springs were important as a water supply and laundry for the Paiutes when Vi was a child. When we came upon the site, however, I was shocked to see a large pump protruding into the middle of the springs! It had been installed

Benton hot springs in 1996.
Photo by the author.

to carry water up to the hot tubs the Bramlettts had built for tourists. Virtually nothing was visible of the original springs. It was nearly impossible to imagine them as they were during Vi's childhood. What a painful disappointment this was.

We walked down a slight incline to the old houses where Vi's family lived. Missing was Mary Ann's house. Harry told us that when Aunt Mary Ann left to live with her son in Bridgeport, she had insisted that her house here in Benton be torn down. Family members tried to dissuade her, but she was adamant. She wanted it down. Neither Harry nor Vi could explain why.

Walking around the ramshackle, old houses, I was overwhelmed by the presence of the people who had once lived there. I walked off to be by myself. Vi noticed and came toward me, saying, "There must be a reason you are off here by yourself." I replied, "Now it's my turn to cry. I can picture that little girl carrying her lard buckets of water from the springs." Vi gave me a hug and said, "It's hard to imagine, isn't it?" I replied, "No, it is very vivid to me. That's why I'm crying." Unlike the hot springs, on this little plot of land there had been no modernizations, no "improvements." Here the past was still tangible.

While we were lingering in the old Indian settlement, Grace remarked that Aunt Mary Ann had an arrowhead-shaped birthmark on her chest, as did Grace's son Gilbert. The two became soul mates. Later, during a late lunch in Bishop, Grace told gambling stories, including ones involving the Paiute Casino, built in 1995, in Bishop. The sixteen-thousand-square-foot gambling house offers poker and blackjack tables, video slots, and poker machines.[7] We discussed the potential impact on Owens Valley of the privately capitalized casino. The Kellers had a wait-and-see attitude, expressing hope that the earnings from gambling that had been allocated for education, housing, and programs for the elderly would actually materialize.

That evening, we visited Viola's sister Winona, who had had a stroke the previous year, at her home on the Bishop reservation. From casual conversation a provocative discussion

Viola Martinez on the trip home in old
Paiute village in Benton, 23 June 1996.
Photo by the author.

emerged regarding membership recognition on the various
Paiute reservations. Winona's daughter, Alberta, argued
strongly that rather than an allotment, she would much prefer
having a piece of property on which she would pay taxes and
which she would really own. She spoke against reservation rules
governing property succession—in particular, that when an
Indian on the reservation dies without a qualified heir, the
deceased's land reverts to the tribe. She also argued that "free"
social services are not good for Indian people.

Viola said she worries that a time might come when natural
resources on the reservations are depleted and cannot keep pace
with population increases. In regard to social services, Vi said
they should be available for both the elderly and for younger
people, with certain restrictions for the latter. She asserted that
those who are able should be required to be self-supporting,
that the time is coming when the youth will be better educated
and opportunities will open up for them.

As I took a photo of Vi and Winona in front of the home they had established on their family allotment, I was moved to tears. I saw them, not as two elderly women, one of whom is impaired by a stroke, but as two young women, raising chickens in the yard in which we were standing to support themselves and Winona's two kids, Alberta and Richard. I also took photos of Vi in front of the storage shed, the roof of which she had shingled herself. Next to Winona's house is Mary Ann's cabin, the one that had been moved from her son's property in Bridge-port so she could be close to Winona and Vi. The little old house is a stark contrast to the modern and exceptionally well-kept mobile home park now operated by Alberta.

After more photos were taken of family members we said our goodbyes. I wondered if I would ever again see these people who had welcomed me into their homes and, more signifi-

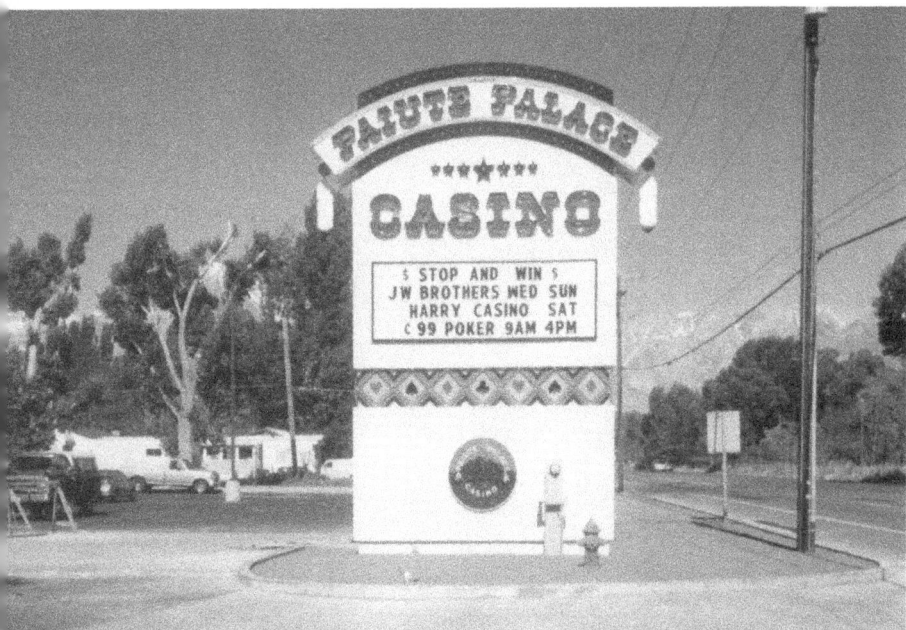

Paiute casino in Bishop.
Photo by the author.

Winona Roach and Viola
Martinez, June 1996.
Photo by the author.

cantly, shared with me their stories, their lives. I feel so privileged to have had this intimate association with Vi's family.

24 June

Since Barbara had decided to remain in Mammoth Lakes a few days longer, Vi and I drove alone to Bishop, where we visited Eleanor at her home. I was captivated by her front walkway, which is laid with stones she has found in the area, including ancient grinding stones. I interviewed her, primarily regarding Sherman Institute. Many of her memories of the boarding school are similar to Vi's, but some of them differ significantly.[8]

> I know I wanted to go [to Sherman Institute]. All you had to do was ask to go and that was it. This was during the depression, of course, and we wanted to go. We were going to a school [in Bishop] at what we called at that time the "Opportunity Class." All Indians. All the Indians stayed together, and all the white kids were in different classes.
>
> This was in 1937. Sure, I wanted to go. These [Sherman Institute] kids, they sounded like they were having fun. It must have been around the third or fourth grade. We lived in the Tee Pee dorm for little kids. It's exciting when you think you are going somewhere, but when you get there, oh God, I was so lonesome. I was so lonesome I remember I used to cry at night.
>
> Then, of course, we had our little duties, so we didn't have time to think about feeling sorry for ourselves. We worked part of the day and then went to school part of the day. We just had things that had to be done.

Although, unlike Vi, Eleanor does not remember being punished for speaking Paiute, she does remember being homesick and lonely the entire time she lived in the Tee Pee dormitory. When she went to the next level, "it was a little easier."

> We used to borrow one another's clothes. None of us had any clothes. Then I had work on the side. I used to have weekend work. One of the teachers, just housework. We

could do that and earn a few dollars. Then I worked in this Beverly Hills home [on outing] for a long time.

We'd come home [to Owens Valley] around Labor Day. Somebody came after us or maybe we took the bus home. Sometimes it was Aunt Nellie [Eleanor's mother's sister]. I remember one time we were all coming home for a few days and we picked up Harry Meredith and Buck Jones [Owens Valley Paiute boys who were students at Sherman Institute}. They were hitchhiking. They were out there in the desert at Red Rock Canyon, sitting by the side of the road. We spotted them and turned around and picked them up. Aunt Nellie had food [in the car], so we fed the boys and had them sit in the back. I was sitting in the rumble seat of the old Ford. I had to squeeze up with the rest of the girls while the two boys sat in the back. We brought them all the way home. They were coming to Bishop, too, from Sherman. They ran away. They ran away from working on the ranch at Sherman.

Now, whenever I meet people from Sherman, everybody just reminisces. We are always so glad to see one another.

Visiting with Eleanor reminded Vi and me of a story, which we had previously recorded in another context, about the first time Vi went to a movie.

As I recall, I went with the Louis Williams family, with my cousin [Eleanor]. When we got there they said, "We have to sit in nigger heaven. That's where the black people go— nigger heaven." I asked what a nigger was, and where is nigger heaven? They told me, "It's way, way up. It's hard to see. You can't see the movie very well." It was just understood that we [Indians] had to go up to nigger heaven. That's where you all sat. But there must have been something in me, because I wouldn't go up there. There were young white girls telling us to go up there. We got up as far as the balcony, and I wouldn't move. All I knew was that it was way up high, and they said you couldn't see. So I wasn't going to go up there. I remember I did get to sit finally. I don't remember how I got a seat, but I know I ended up sitting down and

Eleanor Bethel and Viola Martinez, June 1996,
retracing some of Mary Ann's old trade route.
Photo by the author.

seeing the movie. I never will forget that. I think I was scared
actually.[9]

Following our visit with Eleanor, Vi and I drove to an area
called Sunland, where, according to Vi, the Paiutes used to camp
and where a Presbyterian church was built to minister to these
Indian people. We could find no visible trace of this church.
There remains, however, a huge archway over the barren desert
land behind which is a Paiute cemetery, part of which dates
back over one hundred years.

Our last stop was the return to the Eastern California
Museum in Independence. Kathy Barnes brought out the
Benton photos and we felt, like the old miners of the Eastern
Sierra, that we had struck gold, albeit of a different sort. Before
us were pictures taken by Burton Frasher around the turn of the
century. The Indian dwellings in the photos are intact. Women

are washing clothes in the hot springs. Viola was able to identify a number of the people in the photos. We both ordered copies of these priceless photos documenting the life that Viola remembers living as a young girl in Owens Valley, a remarkable ending to our memorable trip.

◆ ◆ ◆

N. Scott Momaday, a Kiowa, has written the following: "Once in his life a man ought to concentrate his mind upon the remembered earth. . . . He ought to give himself up to a particular landscape in his experience, to look at it from as many angles as he can, to wonder about it, to dwell upon it. . . . I am interested in the way a man looks at a given landscape and takes possession of it in his blood and brain."[10] I am grateful to have gotten a glimpse during our trip of how Viola took possession of Owens Valley in her blood and brain.

In Los Angeles the following morning I found a message from Viola on my voice mail: "I was sitting here thinking of our trip and of my life and realizing that I am blessed. Thank you for the trip."

Conclusion
Culturally Enlarged Elder

Viola's ability to take the lumps inherent in finding opportunity in marginality and becoming "culturally enlarged" was brought home to her during a meeting with young students at Santa Monica City College. A number of the students confided in her as a respected elder that they might have Indian heritage and yearned to trace it but had no means of doing so. Vi has expressed how fortunate she is to have the certainty that she is Paiute and to have a connection to the people and the land. She maximized her boarding school experience to master knowledge of the white world, while striving to maintain her Indianness. She says, "I can imagine that a lot of people who went to boarding school came out of that experience ashamed of their Indianness and therefore disappeared into the white society."[1]

Viola did not disappear into assimilation. "The search or struggle for a sense of ethnic identity," anthropologist Michael M. J. Fischer argues, "is a (re-)invention and discovery of a vision, both ethical and future-oriented."[2] Vi created an ethical vision that looked to the future while drawing on the past. In her eighteen-year teaching career, in her involvement with the American Indian Education Commission and the Native American Ministry, and in her personal life, she dedicated herself to helping whites become more aware of the realities of the lives of Indian people. Assuming the responsibility of this vision meant expanding her cognitive world.

In a paper prepared for an education course in 1969, Viola wrote the following: "My goal through the years, was eventually to return to my people to help them in adapting to the white culture. However, when I did go back, I found I was unable to speak my native language. I was unfamiliar with the customs and traditions of my people and unacceptable because of my Anglo-oriented education and training."[3] She had been displaced from land and culture, even from kin. With great effort and persistence, she did reconnect.

"I can only go onward by going back to where my memories began," writes Joseph Bruchac, who is Abenaki and Slovak.[4] Viola has found her way back to where her memories begin. These memories, related in her narration, confirm her connections with the culture and history of Owens Valley and, more significantly, her links with the complex kinship of her people.

Momaday affirms, "Our best destiny is to imagine, at least, completely who and what and *that* we are. . . . An Indian is an idea which a given man has of himself. And it is a moral idea, for it accounts for the way in which he reacts to other men and to the world in general. And that idea, in order to be realized completely, has to be expressed."[5] How did Viola imagine herself and express this idea: a victim of her boarding school experience? a domestic servant in a white home, the job for which she had been trained? an individual whose brain was inferior to a white person's brain? Clearly she saw herself as a well-educated Indian woman, an educator of both white and Indian children, an individual motivated by her own imagination and determination. Momaday has also written that "the sense of place and the sense of belonging are bonded fast in the imagination."[6] Now the sun always comes up in the right place for Viola. Whether she is in Owens Valley or in Los Angeles, she has a sense of belonging.

What did Viola learn as a child and young woman that she can teach as an elder? Her response to this question is "helping my people understand white society and enlightening white people about the realities of the lives of Indian people." Vi is keenly aware of her reputation and her responsibilities in both white and Indian cultures. As a revered elder in Los Angeles, Viola is engaged in creative and dynamic "sociostructural *bricolage*,"[7] a process by which she creates new constructs from her familiarity with Indian and white, old and new, lifestyles.

In regard to the relationship between what a man is and what he says, Momaday states, "The relationship is both tenuous and complicated. . . . Man has consummate being in language, and there only."[8] There is no remedy for the loss of Vi's native language, a profound consequence of her boarding school years which has forced her to rely on English to revisit her memories. Yet, when she accepted the need to be educated in English, she expanded her margins to master the language: "If I didn't learn anything else I was going to excel in English." With this determination she positioned herself in a potent marginality, one in which she affirms human potential.

The full spectrum of Indian students' responses to boarding schools has yet to be explored.[9] Although the demise of many pre–World War II boarding school students has diminished the opportunities, oral history can nevertheless contribute to a reinterpretation of marginality. Is Vi's story unique? In the Sherman Institute yearbook of 1932, her junior year, Viola Meroney is described as follows: "For her own person, it beggared all description." Indian teenagers quoting Shakespeare to express the distinctiveness of a classmate—I would like to hear their stories.

Literature Review

EVERY LIFE STORY IS UNIQUE, BUT VIOLA'S RECOUNTING OF HER
memories of the greater part of the twentieth century is highly
unusual. In only one other publication is there a depiction of
the American Indian–Japanese American encounters in the War
Relocation Authority internment camps.[1] Despite its unique-
ness, Viola's life history relates closely to other autobiographies
of American Indian women in significant ways, particularly the
impact of white education and the threat of cultural alienation.

In an effort to place Viola's story in context, the following life
histories are reviewed here: *Apache Mothers and Daughters,* by
Ruth McDonald Boyer and Narcissus Duffy Gayton (1992);
Halfbreed, by Maria Campbell (1973); *Lakota Woman,* by Mary
Crow Dog and Richard Erdoes (1990); *Life Lived Like a Story:
Three Yukon Native Elders,* by Julie Cruickshank (1990); *Essie's
Story: The Life and Legacy of a Shoshone Teacher,* by Esther
Burnett Horne and Sally McBeth (1998); *Mankiller, A Chief and
Her People,* by Wilma Mankiller and Michael Wallis (1994);
Molly Spotted Elk: A Penobscot in Paris, by Bunny McBride
(1995); *Mountain Wolf Woman, Sister of Crashing Thunder: The
Autobiography of a Winnebago Indian,* by Mountain Wolf
Woman, edited by Nancy O. Lurie (1966); *No Turning Back: A
True Account of a Hopi Girl's Struggle to Bridge the Gap between
the World of Her People and the World of the White Man,* by
Polingaysi Quoyawayma, as told to Vada F. Carlson (1964);
Karnee: A Paiute Narrative, by Lalla Scott (1966); *A Pima Past,*
by Anna Moore Shaw (1974); *A Voice in Her Tribe: A Navajo
Woman's Own Story,* by Irene Stewart (1980); *Madonna Swan:
A Lakota Woman's Story,* by Madonna Swan as told to Mark

St. Pierre (1991); *Me and Mine: The Life Story of Helen Sekaquap-tewa*, by Sekaquaptewa, as told to Louise Udall (1969).

In each of these life stories, white education is alien territory into which the women are thrust at a very young age. As in Viola's story, the women in ten of these works attended boarding schools, a powerful dynamic in their struggle for ethnic identity.

In *Apache Mothers and Daughters*, a four-generation biography of Chiricahua Apache women, Narcissus, fourth generation, eventually was able to integrate white education with the teachings of her grandmother and great-grandmother. Descriptions of the Santa Fe Indian Boarding School and the Mescalero Agency Boarding School, both in New Mexico, are provided in third-person fictionalized style. Narcissus, like Viola, struggled to attain higher education. After graduating from the Practical Nurses School of the Kiowa Indian Hospital in Oklahoma, she served her tribe as a registered nurse.

Mary Crow Dog, a Lakota, found nothing of value in the Catholic Missionary School in Saint Francis, South Dakota. She characterized it as "unspeakable" and "a curse on our family for generations."[2] After a struggle with alcoholism and alienation, she rediscovered tribal pride through political activism in the American Indian Movement.

In sharp contrast, Mountain Wolf Woman was dismayed when her Winnebago family took her out of the Lutheran Mission School in Wittenberg, Wisconsin. "Alas, I was enjoying school so much and they made me stop. They let me go to school and now they made me quit."[3] Her family arranged her marriage, and she returned to a traditional life; but in her autobiography she expresses regret at not being able to stay in school.

In *No Turning Back*, Polingaysi, a Hopi, was so envious of the children in her village who were going to Sherman Institute that she tried to stow away in the wagon taking the children to the train. In *Me and Mine*, Helen, also a Hopi, had to be taken from her family, who, in opposition to government interference, tried to hide her. At Phoenix Indian Boarding School in Arizona, Helen was so anxiety-ridden she suffered stomach cramps for years. Similarly, shortly after arriving at Sherman Institute, Polingaysi's eagerness was replaced by fear and loneliness. Both women's distress gave way to acceptance of white culture, which eventually led to alienation from their traditional homes. Helen finally reconciled white influence with Hopi traditions by focusing on rural family life and spiritual ceremony. Polingaysi, like Viola, became a teacher, devoted to instructing Indian students about white ways and white students about Indian cultures.

Life Lived Like a Story chronicles the lives of three Yukon elders, one of whom, Angela Sidney, attended the Anglican Chooutla School in Carcross in southern Yukon, Canada. Angela was ambivalent about her experiences at Chooutla. She was excited about going to school until she learned that she would be punished for speaking Tlingit. When her father withdrew her after less than two years, she was distressed because she had not quite learned to read. She valued learning English so much she taught herself by studying whatever books she could find. Her exposure to white education resulted in an intellectual struggle to balance traditional and white ways. Although this struggle never completely ended, she reconciled conflicts by making narrative connections between events in her past and her present life.

Anna Moore Shaw relates in *A Pima Past* how the Gila Crossing reservation day school prepared her for Tucson Indian Boarding School and later the federal government Phoenix Indian School, both in Arizona. Other than admitting homesickness and a mild resentment of the military regime at the Phoenix School, her account of boarding school is neutral. Following graduation from Phoenix, she, like Viola, earned a high school diploma. Unlike Viola, she did not continue her education. Strongly influenced by white culture, she lived in Phoenix for forty years before her husband convinced her to return to the Salt River Pima Reservation. There she realized, "We must retrieve our Pima heritage before it is lost completely."[4] Subsequently she dedicated her time, energy, and education to improving living conditions on the reservation.

In *A Voice in Her Tribe*, Irene Stewart, a Navajo, provides a very sketchy depiction of her four years at Haskell Institute, the federal Indian boarding school in Lawrence, Kansas. As with other boarding school students, her account is ambivalent: she was homesick and physically quite ill at first, but many years later came to appreciate the education she received. "The one thing I have never stopped regretting was not having gone back to Haskell to finish high school. I lost quite a big opportunity by not returning to that fine school."[5] She committed herself to helping her people through intense involvement in the Chinle, Arizona, chapter of the Navajo Tribal Council, serving as secretary and arbiter of disputes.

Lucy Swan, a devout Catholic, sent her daughter Madonna to Immaculate Conception Mission School in Stephan, South Dakota. In *Madonna Swan: A Lakota Woman's Story*, Madonna describes her intense homesickness. Her account of boarding school is overshadowed, however, by a chronicle of her determination to survive tuberculosis. She not only survived, she attended courses at Black Hills State College in South Dakota and became a teacher. Using her white education to help Sioux children on the reservation, she taught in the Cheyenne River HeadStart program for ten years.

The portrayal of boarding school most comparable to Vi's is that of Esther Burnett Horne in *Essie's Story: The Life and Legacy of a Shoshone Teacher*. Upon arrival at Haskell Institute, Essie was "grief-stricken and frightened . . . feeling lost and alone. . . . I thought: 'I hate this place; I will never be happy here.'"[6] As did Vi, Essie came to appreciate the diverse backgrounds of the students. Unlike Vi, Essie is grateful for the school's military regimen, nearly identical to that at Sherman Institute, because it taught self-discipline. Students at Haskell, as at Sherman, attended church every Sunday, but Essie did not puzzle over religion as Viola did.

Like Viola, Essie realized that the boys had more freedom than the girls; and she also spent her spare time reading. She, too, observed that the students' work kept the school operating. On her outing job Essie witnessed an incident of prejudice toward her employer's black laundress. She does not discuss, however, experiences, positive or negative, in the outing system that related directly to her.

Essie explicitly states her approval of Haskell: "My recollections are that in general we were pretty happy; by and large we were like one big happy family."[7] Her sister Bernice had a dramatically different response. "Bernice did not stay at Haskell more than a couple of years. She couldn't adjust to the school. She was so homesick she was physically ill much of the time and they finally sent her home."[8]

The most significant difference between the boarding school experiences of Viola and Essie is that Haskell employed two Native teachers, Ella Deloria and Ruth Muskrat Bronson. These teachers had a profound impact on Essie's life. "When Ruth would tell us to have pride in who we were, she'd say: 'Indians are people, too. Don't forget that.'"[9] Essie emphasizes the importance of their influence: "They wanted us to be proud of who we were as Indian people and as boarding school students but also to be comfortable in explaining our identity to the non-Indian world."[10] Essie, like Viola, devoted her professional life to teaching, motivated, in large part, by her memories of Haskell Institute.

In four of these autobiographies the subjects attended white schools other than boarding schools. Although Maria Campbell, in *Halfbreed*, describes a brief stay at a boarding school in Beauval, Saskatchewan, her memory is so dim, the description adds little to the literature. She does not remember reading or schoolwork, only that she was locked in a dark closet for speaking Cree.

When a school was built in Spring River, three miles from home, Maria, a Métis, attended with white children. Although she says this school was "heaven compared to the residential school," her descriptions of experiences there are grim. "Lunch hours were really rough, because we had not realized until then, the difference in our diets." White students were given "white or brown bread, boiled eggs, apples, cakes, cookies, and jars of milk." The "halfbreed" children had bannock spread with lard and gopher meat. They were teased mercilessly by the white students. "We fought back, of course, but we were terribly hurt and above all, ashamed. I remember coming home and saying ugly things to Mom . . . I hated her, Daddy, and 'all of you no-good Halfbreeds.'"[11]

Maria's painful conflict regarding her ethnic identity continues for years. Her rootless existence is complicated by drug addiction and alcoholism. She finds her way back to traditional values by remembering the indomitable spirit of Cheechum, her great-grandmother. The narration does not end with a reconciliation of her white and Cree identities, but rather with a vow: "Change will come because this time we [Métis] won't give up."[12]

Annie Lowry, a Northern Paiute, paints a benign picture of her school experiences in *Karnee: A Paiute Narrative*. She claims that she was the first Indian in Lovelock, Nevada, to go to school with white children. "Perhaps I was the first person of the Paiute tribe to go to school at all." However, the editor of *Karnee*, Lalla Scott, states in a note that Sarah Winnemucca Hopkins probably had this honor.[13]

Annie relates one negative experience, the result of her winning a spelling bee. A white mother was so incensed she complained: "I know that little Paiute is not smarter than my girl. She ought not to be in school anyway. . . . Why don't they put her out." Annie's white father settles the matter quickly and forcefully by reminding school authorities that he is one of the biggest taxpayers in the district. Annie laments that when her father left her mother, she never went to school again.

In *Molly Spotted Elk: A Penobscot in Paris,* Molly has a distinctive history of encounters with white education. Living with her family on Indian Island, Maine, she attended school on the island through the sixth grade. An opportunity to continue her education was available at the cost of attending Old Town Junior High School with white students across the Penobscot River. White students' harassment of Indian students was so relentless most of the Indians quit. Molly stuck it out and graduated.

She registered for high school in 1917 at age thirteen; but because she had to help support her family by working as a governess, she was not able to attend until 1920. She had been so strongly influenced by white education she dreamed of becoming a writer; but after two terms in high school, she ventured into show business. Subsequent education was experiential and inextricably tied to her work as a performer, which took her to Paris and a much wider, more worldly education.

In her autobiography Wilma Mankiller discusses the impact of boarding schools on two previous generations of Cherokees, including her father's experience. Her assessment of these schools is unconditionally negative: "mental and physical abuse occurred." She claims that widespread sexual abuse of young men in boarding schools has been documented.[14] Her own schooling from first through fifth grades was at Rocky Mountain School, three miles from her home in Mankiller Flats, Oklahoma. She relates only one mildly negative incident when she was teased by white girls for her flour-sack underwear. In the 1960s her family relocated to San Francisco under the auspices of the federal Termination and Relocation program. After a year they bought a house in Daly City, south of San Francisco, where Wilma entered the seventh grade. She reacted to this public school as did many students entering boarding schools: "I hated school. I hated the teachers. I hated the other students. Most of all, I hated the city."[15] She regains equilibrium by spending a year with her grandmother on a farm, then returns to the city, finishes high school, and eventually earns an undergraduate degree from San Francisco State College.

Mankiller is the most politically active of the women in these autobiographies. In 1969 she became intensely involved in the American Indian takeover of Alcatraz Island, a former penitentiary off the coast of San Francisco: "The occupation of Alcatraz . . . was extremely liberating for me. As a result, I consciously took a path I still find myself on today as I continue to work for the revitalization of tribal communities."[16] This involvement led her back to the Cherokee Nation, of which she became principal chief in 1985.

Urbanization, a decisive factor in Wilma's life as in Viola's, is significant in five of the life histories, including *Mankiller*. These works present diverse perspectives on urbanization. In *Apache Mothers and Daughters*, although the city is portrayed as neutral, it is important as a place for employment. In contrast, Maria Campbell in *Halfbreed* finds the city severely alienating, leading her to drug and alcohol abuse. In *Molly Spotted Elk*, city life is inseparable from Molly's career in show business. Like Viola, Anna Moore Shaw in *A Pima Past* has urban experiences that allow her to become culturally enlarged and eventually to return to her rural reservation without displacement.

Like Viola, five of the women—Esther Horne, Anna Moore Shaw, Madonna Swan, Polingaysi Qoyawayma, and Helen Sekaquaptewa—chose a teaching career as the most effective way to integrate traditional values with white education.

All of the women in these autobiographies had to make critical decisions in order to adapt to the dramatic changes in their lives. Their adaptations required strength and courage. Each woman responded in her unique way, drawing on early traditional exposure as she positioned herself in twentieth-century white society.

Structure and methodology differ considerably among the works reviewed. Two of the works appear to have been written without collaboration, Maria Campbell's *Halfbreed* and *A Pima Past* by Anna Moore Shaw. Gretchen M. Bataille and Kathleen Mullen Sands write about bicultural composite authorship in

American Indian Women Telling Their Lives. "While some auto-biographies by Indian people have been written solely by the author, even those have in some measure gone through bicul-tural processing in preparation of the manuscript for publica-tion for a primarily non-Indian audience."[17]

Neither of these autobiographies gives information as to bicultural processing. Shaw, in this personal narrative and cultural memoir, uses a fictional third-person style when writing about family history and first-person narrative when writing about her own history. The book is without analysis, notes, or index. *Halfbreed* is a convincing personal confession, probably with minimal, if any, processing through an editor. Maria's personal insights constitute the only analysis. There are no notes or index.

Apache Mothers and Daughters leaves no doubt as to collab-oration. Boyer and Gayton worked together for thirty-five years, collecting remembrances and shaping them into a fictionalized account. Boyer supports Narcissus Gayton's oral history with scholarly fieldwork. The third-person narrative technique is sometimes dramatic but often distracting. Some-times it is difficult to discriminate between fact and fiction.

Lakota Woman, like *Halfbreed,* is a first-person confessional with no scholarly analysis. Mary Crow Dog and Richard Erdoes are credited as coauthors, but no information is provided about their collaboration.

Julie Cruickshank's admirable and extremely effective struc-ture takes full advantage of the three narrators' material, alter-nating traditional stories with complementary personal narratives. Cruickshank provides considerable information as to precisely how the collaborations worked.

Wilma Mankiller and Michael Wallis are named as co-authors of their book, but they give little information about their collaboration. Wilma thanks Wallis for his "great work." Wallis declares, "The writing of the work was a true collabora-tion in every sense of the word. I will always cherish the memory of those long sessions spent at Wilma's home as we wove the fabric and fiber that make up the story of this remarkable woman's life."[18]

Bunny McBride collaborated not with Molly Spotted Elk but with her diaries, extraordinary documents of both private and public experiences. The author supplements the diaries with interviews, letters, secondary sources, and her own explorations of Indian Island, New York, and Paris, where Molly had lived. The third-person narrative is appropriate for the material, but, as with *Apache Mothers and Daughters*, the reader is sometimes not clear whose thoughts are being presented.

Nancy Oestrich Lurie, editor of *Mountain Wolf Woman*, thoroughly explains her collaboration with Mountain Wolf Woman, her Winnebago relative by adoption. This relationship allowed the collaboration to happen, as Winnebago Indians have a strong sense of obligation to relatives. The preface describes how the two women worked together to produce the oral history. Lurie offers additional information in two appendices: appendix A, containing the unedited version of Mountain Wolf Woman's narration; and appendix B, the edited version with Lurie's commentary.

No Turning Back provides no information regarding the collaboration between Polingaysi Qoyawayma (Elizabeth White) and her as-told-to editor Vada F. Carlson. Although the reader assumes that Polingaysi is the author, the story is told in third person, distancing the reader from this very personal account.

The collaboration that produced *Karnee: A Paiute Narrative* is reasonably explained in the preface, by Robert F. Heizer, and the commentary and notes, provided by Charles R. Craig. One would have liked comments by the editor, Lalla Scott, regarding how she worked with her subject, Annie Lowry. The book has two distinct parts. The first, dealing with Annie's mother Sau-Tau-nee, is subjective in tone, while the second is considerably more objective. Craig suggests the shift in tone may be due to a seven-year lapse between the writing of the first and second parts.

A Voice in Her Tribe: A Navajo Woman's Own Story had a rather unusual collaboration: Irene Stewart told her story in letters to the editor, Mary Shepardson. The letters were further edited by Doris Ostrander Dawdy. In the foreword Shepardson notes, "Some of the spelling and grammar has been changed in order to give the reader a better sense of the status Irene occupies in her own society and culture. But Mrs. Dawdy has, I feel, been able quite successfully to preserve the flavor of Irene's speech and personality."[19] The work includes traditional Navajo stories, reflections on tribal politics, and descriptions of Navajo social behavior, all related in first-person narrative. The narrative lacks energy, though; perhaps Irene's personality has not been preserved in the editing.

Madonna Swan: A Lakota Woman's Story is told through Mark St. Pierre, who has lived among the Lakota people since 1971. He explains the unusual collaboration in the preface: "Between 1975 and 1981 I recorded triplicate versions of these stories, and in the writing process edited the stories into a unified vignette, pulling the best aspects from the three versions. My next challenge was to add settings where needed and to write them in such a manner that the colloquial manner of the telling was left intact and had the proper mood and feeling."[20] Although the first-person narrative flows fairly well, one wonders if spontaneity was lost in the integration of the three versions.

Me and Mine: The Life Story of Helen Sekaquaptewa is told to Louise Udall. Since it was intended as the story of Helen's life for her grandchildren, it is a first-person memoir with no analysis, notes, or bibliography. Helen summarized her collaboration with Udall: "I am talking. She is writing."

The editing of *Essie's Story*, according to Sally McBeth, occupied hundreds of hours of work and companionship over a ten-year period. "We both edited every page." This collaborative editing came at a cost. McBeth admits: "I believe much of [Essie's] warmth and humor and her thoughtful reflections have been lost in the writing process."[21]

After reviewing these life histories of American Indian women, each of whom has a unique and dramatic story to tell, I became convinced that the author's primary responsibility is to assure that the narrator's individual voice is heard. While I greatly admire the seamless collaboration achieved by Horne and McBeth, I was unwilling to risk losing Vi's spontaneity, humor, and perceptive insights in order to achieve a similar fusion.

Bataille and Sands argue, "It is the job of the editor to order fragmented experience in time and in relation to narrative viewpoint and intention."[22] I saw this ordering as my responsibility in writing the story Viola was telling. Our method was an integration of first-person narration and historical context. I tape-recorded each session. Viola directed the story, I provided the broader historical context. We reviewed each interview during the following session, both of us clarifying and enriching that segment of Vi's story. We used a similar procedure when Vi reviewed the first draft of the manuscript. When questions or uncertainty arose, Viola had ultimate authority. She owns the story.

Viola's and my collaboration, which has resulted in this volume, has been enriched by our personal relationship, beginning with our meeting ten years ago, appropriately, at a wedding. Both our friendship and our work together have been strengthened by frequent telephone conversations, mutual involvement with the LAUSD American Indian Education Commission, get-togethers with our families, and the memorable trip to Owens Valley. Viola has trusted me to convey her life story with authenticity and sensitivity. This book is my response to her trust, a testimony to the significance of her individual experiences, which illuminate nine decades of California history.

Afterword

2003

VIOLA'S STORY IS ONE OF LOSS AND RECOVERY. THE LITERATURE on American Indian women with similar experiences includes phrases such as "navigating unfamiliar waters without channel markers";[1] "struggling for survival on several planes—intellectual, emotional, physical, and spiritual";[2] experiencing the rupture of the "intricate tapestry of interconnections" leading to a rupture in "the entire fabric of one's identity";[3] and "trying to walk this path in balance without losing oneself in the process."[4]

During the creation of this book my son, Timothy, died suddenly and unexpectedly. Descriptions of my passage through grief include navigating a white river of emotions with no shoreline in sight; recovering from a shattered heart even the tiniest fragments—precious, essential components in the rebuilding of an identity; feeling confusion and fear in a world suddenly lacking all familiar landmarks; trying to keep the heart open, to maintain some loving balance in the face of traumatic pain and confusion.

As Vi's story unfolded, I realized that each of us has the potential to transform loss into grace, and confusion into insight, even wisdom. Storytelling has the power to transform both the teller and the listener. By recounting and listening, Vi and I have mutually eased the journey, not from loss to resolution, but from loss to reconcialiation.

2010

Viola Meroney Martinez died on February 3, 2010. A service celebrating her life was held on March 13 at St. John's Presbyterian Church in Los Angeles, where Viola had served as a Sunday School teacher, deacon, and elder. The service was conducted by Pastor Steven Craig.

An emotional eulogy was given by Robert Augular, whose relationaship with Viola grew so close that Vi considered him a family member. When she became fragile during her last years, Augular was a primary caretaker. Ed Keener, a friend for more than thirty years, spoke about the joyful times his family shared with Viola and her family. Vianne Wentzell, Viola's daughter, reminisced about her mother's gentle, loving, and generous spirit. In my eulogy I recalled memories of Viola in her own words, recorded in her life history.

The church was filled to capacity with a balance of Indians and non-Indians, confirming that after years of great effort and persistence in both Indian and white cultures, Viola had become a revered elder in both societies. Ultimately, whether she was in Los Angeles or Owens Valley, she had a sense of belonging, of being home, and the sun always came up in the right place for her.

Notes

Introduction

1. Leonard Freedman, interview by the author, University of California at Los Angeles (UCLA), 3 March 1999.

2. Stonequist [1937] 1961, xv.

3. Clifton 1989, 28–29.

4. Hertzberg 1971, 19.

5. Szasz 1994, 8; Mihesuah 1996a, 22; 1996b, 92–95; Coleman 1993, 3–11.

6. Adams 1995; Berg 1989; Child 1999; Coleman 1993; Horne and McBeth 1998.

7. McFee 1968, 309–10; Bahr, Chadwick, and Day 1972, 109–10.

8. Clifton 1989, 29.

9. Katz 1995, 3.

10. Momaday 1975, 103, 97.

11. Clifton 1989, ix.

12. Interview 11, 1 May 1996, 35. Numbered interviews refer to interviews conducted by the author from 31 January 1996 to 24 March 1997. Interviews were of Viola Martinez, unless otherwise indicated. Transcripts of the interviews are in the possession of the author.

13. Karst 1995, 311.

14. Interview 11, 1 May 1996, 30.

15. Vianne Martinez Wentzell, interview 20, 11 February 1997, 9.

16. Allen 1986, 129–30.

17. Bahr 1995, 10.

18. Karst 1995, 369.

19. Walton 1992, 14.

20. Chalfant 1993; Burton and Wehrey 1996; and Unrau 1996. An excellent account of Indian-white conflict in Owens Valley, including ethnographic reports by Paiutes, can be found in Walton 1992, 18–22.

21. Unrau 1996, 139.

22. Quoted in ibid., 140.

23. Ibid., 147; Burton and Wehrey 1996, 124.

24. Bataille and Sands 1984, 94.

25. Hertzberg 1971, 20.

26. Young 1987, 78.

27. Adams 1995, 266.

28. Garrod and Larimore 1997, 3.

29. Cook-Lynn 1996, 57.

30. Liberty 1978, 136.

31. I am indebted to Straus and Valentino 1998 for providing a dynamic model for research on Indians in the city.

32. Fixico 1986, 36.

33. Kelly 1988, 76.

34. Bahr 1995, 14.

35. Michael McLaughlin, librarian, American Indian Resource Center, Huntington Park, Calif., telephone conversation with the author, 15 October 2001.

36. Bahr 1995, 14.

37. Lobo 1998, 91.

38. The discussion of the development of the Native American Ministry of the Presbyterian Church in Los Angeles is informed by interview 14; by communications between the church and its congregants, whose documents are in the possession of Viola Martinez; and by Burgess and Johnson 2000.

Chapter 1

1. Viola has no written record of her birth. Oral tradition places her birth in 1917.

2. Interview 8, 10 April 1996, 23–24.

3. Smith 1993, 194.

4. Liljeblad and Fowler 1986, 412.

5. Ibid., 418; Unrau 1996, 135.

6. Walton 1982, 14.

7. Vernon Miller, tribal chairman, Fort Independence, Calif., telephone conversation with the author, 14 June 2000.

8. Liljeblad and Fowler 1986, 412; Walter 1986, 32.

9. Liljeblad and Fowler 1986, 413.

10. Unrau 1996, 136.

11. Smith 1993, 199; Burton and Wehrey 1996, 123; Chalfant, 98; Walton 1982, 14.

12. Unrau 1996, 138, emphasis added.

13. Unrau 1996, 142–43.

14. DeDecker 1966, 25, 27.

15. Interview 4, 21 February 1996, 20–24.

16. Cook 1976b, 452.

17. Burton and Wehrey 1996, 126.

18. Hundley argues: "The adoption of agriculture would have required no great cultural leap for the Paiute. Always in close touch with their environment, the food-conscious Natives of Owens Valley could not have helped but notice that the naturally occurring nutritious plants grew in more abundance in the marshlands and in areas along creeks subject to occasional overflow. It would have been a short step to watering promising lands artificially." (1992, 16–18)

19. Ibid., 4.

20. Kahrl 1983, 32–33.

21. Smith 1993, 206–207.

22. "The Owens Irony," B7.

23. Burton and Wehrey 1996, 145.

24. "The Owens Irony," B7.

25. Walton 1982, 206

26. Hundley 1992, 164.

27. A thorough discussion of the Land Exchange Act of 1937 is presented in Walter 1986.

28. For an excellent discussion of Native adaptation in the Great Basin, see Knack 1987.

29. Interview 5, 6 March 1996, 6–7.

30. Interview 3, 14 February 1996, 22–25. Documentation of individual children being stolen from their Indian families probably exists only in family oral history or personal papers. The novel *Indian Killer* by Sherman Alexi (1996) is based on the fictional story of a newborn Indian baby being stolen from his mother and given to a white couple. That Alexi has chosen this experience, the theft by whites of an Indian child, to explore alienation and lost heritage indicates the presence of such tales in the oral history.

According to Professor Carole Goldberg, UCLA School of Law, there is a significant record of cases of involuntary termination of parental rights of Indian parents based on alleged abuse and neglect and of adoption proceedings in state courts undertaken without adequately informed consent or opportunity for retraction by the Indian parents. A pattern of such cases led to the enactment in 1978 of the Indian Child Welfare Act. Among its provisions are those of providing jurisdiction of Indian tribes in child custody proceedings and assurance that the child is placed in an Indian cultural environment. Carole Goldberg, e-mail to the author, 2 October 2001.

Chapter 2

1. Interview 3, 14 February 1996, 29.

2. Knack 1980, 52, 67.

3. Viola Martinez, telephone conversation with the author, 26 March 1999.

4. National Archives, RG 75.

5. Field notes, 4 February 1997.

6. Field notes, 10 March 1996.

7. Interview 3, 14 February 1996, 31–32.

8. In Viola's file in the National Archives her application for enrollment in Sherman Institute designates her father as "Sullivan Meroeny [sic], dead."

9. Wheat explains this relationship: because two or more Paiute sisters frequently married the same man, the children of different mothers call each other sister-cousin. (1967, 113)

10. Interview 3, 14 February 1996, 30.

11. Interview 16, 12 June 1996, 18, 19.

12. Ibid., 15.

13. Interview 5, 6 March 1996, 8, 9, 11.

14. Vianne Martinez Wentzell, interview 20, 11 February 1997, 5.

15. Sheila is related to Viola through Tom Gustie. Their both having the surname Martinez is coincidental.

16. Interview 22, 24 March 1997, 17–18.

17. Interview 16, 12 June 1996, 22, 23.

18. Interview 3, 14 February 1996, 33.

19. Interview 4, 21 February 1996, 10–12.

20. Potashin, 3–5.

21. Spence, 46–47.

22. Interview 3, 14 February 1996, 33–36.

23. Interview 16, 12 June 1996, 20–22.

24. Field notes, 25 June 1996.

25. Field notes, 26 June 1996.

26. Interview 3, 14 February 1996, 35–36.

27. Interview 9, 25 April 1996, entire interview.

28. Interview 9, 25 April 1996, 1–17.

29. Vianne Martinez Wentzell, interview 20, 11 February 1997, 3; Kirk Martinez, interview 23, 31 May 1997, 3.

30. Sheila Gustie Martinez, interview 22, 24 March 1997, 12, 13.

31. Interview 9, 25 April 1996, 22.

32. See chap. 9, "The Trip Home."

33. Interview 1, 31 January 1996, 21.

34. Coleman 1993; Child 1999; Adams 1995.

35. Interview 8, 10 April 1996, 16, 22.

36. Ibid., 19.

37. Ibid., 13.

38. Interview 8, 10 April 1996, 21.

39. Viola Martinez, telephone conversation with the author, 18 July 2000.

40. Interview 8, 10 April 1996, 30–31.

Chapter 3

1. For a comprehensive history of the federal boarding schools see Reyhner and Eder 1992, 33–58.

2. Child 1999; Coleman 1993; Lomawaima, Adams 1995; McBeth 1983.

3. Simons 1942, 117.

4. Qoyawayma 1964, 59.

5. Interview 8, 10 April 1996, 33–36.

6. Sherman Institute *Smudgepot* 1931, 26.

7. Miller 1996, 290.

8. Interview 10, 25 April 1996, 24.

9. Ibid., 26.

10. Interview 1, 31 January 1996, 33–34.

11. Miller 1996, 428.

12. Interview 8, 10 April 1996, 39.

13. Adams 1995, 117.

14. Interview 13, 8 May 1996, 39–42.

15. Ibid., 35–38.

16. Coleman 1993, 119; Adams 1995, 23, 164; Child 1999, 79.

17. Interview 13, 8 May 1996, 22–25.

18. Ibid., 27–31.

19. Viola's religious growth is discussed in chapter 7.

20. Victoria Patterson points out that Indians are the only ethnic group in the United States that has a specific educational policy. (1989, 32)

21. Prucha 1973, 221, 224.

22. Interview 1, 31 January 1996, 13, 14; interview 8, 10 April 1996, 41–44.

23. Interview 11, 1 May 1996, 22.

24. Interview 8, 10 April 1996, 46.

25. Coleman 1993, 109.

26. Interview 11, 1 May 1996, 30.

27. Ibid., 35.

28. Hertzberg believes that Pratt's prejudices were cultural rather than racial: "To him, the Indian was a man like other men. He rejected utterly all notions of inborn racial inferiority. To Pratt, the problem was to strip the Indian of his Indianness and to replace this with a new set of religious and social attitudes and skills in harmony with the larger society." (1971, 16–17)

29. Prucha 1973, 35.

30. Ibid., 274.

31. Child 1999, 81.

32. Adams 1995, 162–63.

33. Trennert 1983, 267.

34. Ibid., 287, n.41.

35. Clara Moorhead Moran, interview 21, 4 March 1997, 47.

36. Ibid., 44–45.

37. Ibid., 49.

38. Interview 6, 21 March 1996, 34.

39. Ibid., 35.

40. Interview 7, 3 April 1996, 6–10; interview 8, 10 April 1996, 1–5.

41. Interview 8, 10 April 1996, 5–7.

42. Interview 6, 21 March 1996, 37–38.

43. Interview 11, 1 May 1996, 30.

44. Coleman in *American Indian Children at School, 1850–1930* concludes, "The complex interplay among motivational influences produced highly individual and ambivalent

responses." (1993, 79)

45. Interview 11, 1 May 1996, 37.

Chapter 4

1. Interview 1, 31 January 1996, 37.

2. Berg 1989, 27.

3. Interview 11, 1 May 1996, 4–5.

4. Coleman 1993, 84; Adams 1995, 266.

5. Interview 5, 6 March 1996, 25–26.

6. Interview 12, 1 May 1996, 8–11.

7. Szasz 1997, 16–36. *The Problem of Indian Administration* (1928) was called the Meriam Report because it was created by the Brookings Institution under the direction of Lewis Meriam. The report, commissioned by Secretary of the Interior Hubert Work, exposed the deficiencies of the

Bureau of Indian Affairs. The section on education, written by W. Carson Ryan, included a penetrating and severe criticism of the federal boarding school system.

8. Viola Martinez, telephone conversation with the author, 1 October 2001.

9. Kidwell 1986, 94.

10. Allen Lovine, also a Sherman Institute graduate, was a Western Shoshone from North Folk in northern Nevada, a group also called "root-diggers" or "diggers."

11. Interview 12, 1 May 1996, 12.

12. National Archives, RG 75, student record of year 1931–32.

13. Ibid., Viola's record from Riverside Junior College, 1933–34.

14. Ibid., letter dated 10 January 1934.

15. Ibid., letter dated 28 June 1934.

16. Ibid., letter dated 23 April 1933. Although not named in the letter, John Collier had been commissioner of Indian affairs for two days.

17. Szasz 1977, 135.

18. National Archives, RG 75, letter dated 1 June 1936.

19. Ibid., letter to Biery from C. F. Rhoads, commissioner of Indian affairs, dated 14 May 1932.

20. Interview 13, 8 May 1996, 7.

21. Ibid., 6–8.

22. Ibid., 12.

23. Interview 3, 14 February 1996, 3–4.

24. Winona Meroney Sherrill Roach died on 1 July 2001 in Bishop.

25. John Cosgrave, interview 2, 7 February 1996, 2–3.

26. Ibid., 6–7.

27. Viola Martinez, telephone conversation with the author, 31 January 2001.

28. Interview 3, 14 February 1996, 6.

29. Viola Martinez, telephone conversation with the author, 31 January 2001.

30. Interview 14, 15 May 1996, 8–11.

31. National Archives, RG 75, letters dated 4 January and 16 February 1937.

32. Ibid., letter dated 9 March 1937.

33. Ibid., letter dated as received by Sherman Institute, 4 February 1937.

34. Hertzberg 1971, 313.

35. National Archives, RG 75, scholarships file, letter dated 24 June 1937.

36. Vianne Martinez Wentzell, interview 20, 11 February 1997, 15.

37. Garrod and Larimore 1997, 2.

38. Szasz 1977, 136.

39. Viola Martinez, telephone conversation with the author, 1 October 2001.

40. Interview 5, 6 March 1996, 27.

41. National Archives, RG 75, letter dated 17 June 1939.

42. Ibid., letter dated 21 May 1940.

43. Interview 3, 14 February 1996, 3.

44. Ibid., 6–7.

45. Ibid., 6–8.

46. Interview 5, 6 March 1996, 29–32.

47. Viola Martinez, interview by the author, not tape-recorded, 10 July 1996.

48. Interview 5, 6 March 1996, 32–33.

49. Interview 3, 14 February 1996, 11.

Chapter 5

1. Hundley 1992, 162–64; Walton 1982, 209, 283; Liljeblad and Fowler 1986, 431.

2. Ibid.; see Walter 1986.

3. Interview 7, 3 April 1996, 2–6.

4. Interview 19, 16 October 1996, 5–7.

5. Interview 1, 31 January 1996, 32; interview 4, 21 February 1996, 38.

6. Interview 19, 16 October 1996, 12.

7. Interview 5, 6 March 1996, 10–14.

8. Ibid., 15–19.

9. Interview 3, 14 February 1996, 19.

10. Interview 19, 16 October 1996, 8–10.

11. Ibid., 14.

12. Interview 14, 15 May 1996, 44.

13. Interview 19, 16 October 1996, 15–19.

14. Interview 3, 14 February 1996, 17–18; interview 5, 6 March 1996, 35–41; interview 6, 21 March 1996, 8–12.

15. John Cosgrave, interview 2, 7 February 1996, 1, 6, 7.

16. Interview 5, 6 March 1996, 35–41.

Chapter 6

1. Unrau 1996, 861.

2. Ibid., 29–30.

3. Manzanar Committee 1998, 3–5.

4. For an overview on the relocation sites, including population statistics, see Burton, Farrell, Lord, and Lord 1999.

5. Manzanar Committee 1998, iii–iv.

6. Sue Kunitomi Embrey, telephone conversation with the author, 11 April 2002.

7. Burton, Farrell, Lord, and Lord 1999, 162–63.

8. Ibid.

9. Van Horn 1995, 28. Despite the fact that the camps were located on or near Indian land, there is very little published research on the interaction of Native Americans and Japanese Americans, other than Okimoto 2001 and National Park Service publications Van Horn 1995 and Unrau 1996.

10. Ibid., 16.

11. Unrau 1996, 761.

12. Ibid., 784.

13. Interview 4, 21 February 1996, 43–44.

14. Ibid., 58; interview 6, 21 March 1996, 2.

15. Unrau 1996, 430.

16. Interview 4, 21 February 1996, 58.

17. U.S. Department of Interior (DOI) War Relocation Authority [hereafter DOI] 1943, 3.

18. Interview 4, 21 February 1996, 59–60.

19. Unrau 1996, 771.

20. Interview 4, 21 February 1996, 39–41.

21. Field notes, Benton, 23 June 1996.

22. Interview 5, 6 March 1996, 42.

23. Interview 4, 21 February 1996, 44.

24. Ibid., 45.

25. Unrau 1996, 534; Adams 1944; Armor and Wright 1988, xvii–xx.

26. Interview 4, 21 February 1996, 63–65.

27. Unrau 1996, 429; Manzanar Committee 1998, 7.

28. Interview 6, 21 March 1996, 14–15.

29. Interview 7, 3 April 1996, 8–9.

30. Interview 6, 21 March 1996, 15.

31. Interview 4, 21 February 1996, 46–47.

32. Cohen, Burton, and Farrell 1996, 42–43.

33. Ibid.

34. Unrau 1996, 756.

35. Interview 4, 21 February 1996, 46–47.

36. DOI 1946.

37. Interview 4, 21 February 1996, 62–66.

38. Interview 5, 6 March 1996, 49.

39. Unrau 1996, 855–57.

40. Ibid., xxv–xxvi.

41. Interview 4, 21 February 1996, 67–68.

Chapter 7

1. Dorris 1987, 98, 103.

2. Interview 16, 12 June 1996, 8.

3. Viola Martinez, telephone conversation with the author, 8 March 2001.

4. For an excellent discussion of this history, see Weibel-Orlando 1991, 12–18.

5. Fixico 1986, 4, 8, 9.

6. Drinnon 1987 is a comprehensive study of parallels between the treatment of Japanese Americans and American Indians under Myer.

7. Hart 1986, 157.

8. Clemmer and Stewart 1986, 550.

9. Viola Martinez, interview with the author, not tape-recorded, 27 March 2001.

10. Interview 14, 15 May 1996, 48.

11. Viola Martinez, 1974, unpublished paper, UCLA.

12. Interview 14, 15 May 1996, 49.

13. Interview 21, 4 March 1997, 67.

14. Interview 5, 6 March 1996, 52; interview 15, 22 May 1996, 2.

15. Interview 5, 6 March 1996, 46.

16. Ibid., 53. Vi was reluctant to talk about the adoptions of her children until she had their consent to do so.

17. Interview 15, 22 May 1996, 4–5.

18. Interview 19, 16 October 1996, 45–46.

19. Interview 4, 21 February 1996, 36; interview 19, 16 October 1996, 45.

20. Statements by Kirk Martinez are extracted from interview 23, 31 May 1997; statements by Vianne Martinez Wentzell are extracted from interview 20, 11 February 1997.

21. For a description of mining activity in the Eastern Sierra, see Smith 1993, 200–205; Unrau 1996, 141–43.

22. Interview 4, 21 February 1996, 26–35.

23. Shoemaker 1988, 431.

24. Interview 18, 10 July 1996, 20.

25. See the Introduction, n.38.

26. The survey found that 64 percent of respondents were interested

in attending Presbyterian services, 82 percent were interested in ecumenical services, 12 percent regularly practiced tribal spiritual ways, and 41 percent occasionally did so. Presbyterian Survey of American Indians in Los Angeles 1989.

27. Interview 22, 24 March 1997, 22–44.

28. Viola Martinez, telephone conversation with the author, 25 March 1997.

Chapter 8

1. Interview 15, 22 May 1996, 5–21.

2. Viane Martinez Wentzell 1990, "Developmental Study," unpublished paper, UCLA, 6.

3. Interview 15, 22 May 1996, 23–40; John Orendorff, interview by the author, 27 September 1998, 1–7.

Chapter 9

1. This chapter relies on field notes taken by the author during the trip and on Smith 1993 for factual and descriptive information about the area traveled.

2. Walton 1982, 70.

3. Mono Lake Schoolhouse Museum, n.d.

4. Smith 1993, 26.

5. Smith 1993, 195; Chalfant 1933, 82–83.

6. Smith 1993, 48–49.

7. Forstenzer 1995, A-3, 24.

8. Interview 17, 25 June 1996.

9. Interview 6, 21 March 1996, 23–26.

10. Momaday 1975, 99, 101.

Conclusion

1. Field notes, 14 March 1996.

2. Fischer 1986, 196.

3. Viola Martinez 1969, "Anglo-oriented Education and Training," unpublished paper, UCLA.

4. Swann and Krupat 1987, 199.

5. Momaday 1975, 103.

6. Momaday 1997, 111.

7. Weibel-Orlando 1991, 7–9.

8. Momaday 1975, 104.

9. Adams 1995, 238.

Literature Review

1. Okimoto 2001.
2. Crow Dog and Erdoes 1990, 30, 31.
3. Mountain Wolf Woman 1966, 29.
4. Shaw 1974, 212.
5. Stewart 1980, 34.
6. Horne and McBeth 1998, 31.
7. Ibid., 36.
8. Ibid., 48.
9. Ibid., 42.
10. Ibid., 49.
11. Campbell 1973, 46–47.
12. Ibid., 157.
13. Lowry 1966, 47, 140.
14. Mankiller and Wallis 1994, 9.
15. Ibid., 103.
16. Ibid., 192.
17. Bataille and Sands 1984, 9.
18. Mankiller and Wallis 1994, x.
19. Stewart 1980, 7.
20. Swan 1991, ix.
21. Horne and McBeth 1998, xvi.
22. Bataille and Sands 1984, 14.

Afterword

1. Katz 1995, 3.
2. Garrod and Larimore 1997, 1.
3. Ibid., 4.
4. Ibid., 1, 2.

Bibliography

Primary Sources

Bethel, Eleanor. 1996. Interview 17 by the author. Bishop, Calif. 25 June.

Cosgrave, John Stanton. 1996. Interview 2 by the author. Beverly Hills, Calif. 7 February.

Eastern California Museum Archives. Documents and photographs relating to Owens Valley, including Manzanar Historic Site and Paiute/Shoshone Indians. Independence, Calif.

Los Angeles American Indian Education Commission. 1976–1996. Records. Los Angeles.

Martinez, Kirkland Robert. 1997. Interview 23 by the author. Los Angeles. 31 May.

Martinez, Sheila Gustie. 1997. Interview 22 by the author. Pasadena, Calif. 24 March.

Martinez, Viola Meroney. 1996. Interviews 1–19 by the author. Los Angeles. 31 January–16 October.

McLaughlin, Michael. 2001. Telephone conversation with the author, 15 October.

Moran, Clara Moorhead Lopez. 1997. Interview 21 by the author. Los Angeles. 4 March.

National Archives Branch Depository, Pacific Southwest Region, Laguna Nigel, California. RG 75 Bureau of Indian Affairs; Agency: Sherman Institute; Series: Student Case Files, 1903–1950; Box 241 (Viola Meroney).

Orendorff, John. 1998. Interview by the author. Reseda, Calif. 27 September.

Sherman Institute Museum Archives. Riverside, Calif.

U.S. Department of the Interior. National Park Service, Pacific West Field area. 1995. *Manzanar National Historic Site, California, Draft of General Management Plan and Environmental Impact Statement.* December. San Francisco.

U.S. Department of the Interior. War Relocation Authority. 1943–1946. *Semi-Annual Reports.* 1 January–30 June 1943; 1 July–31 December 1944; 1 January–30 June 1945; July 1–December 31, 1946. Washington, D.C.: GPO.

Wentzell, Vianne Lynn Martinez. 1997. Interview 20 by the author. Camarillo, Calif. 11 February.

Secondary Sources

Adams, Ansel. 1944. *Born Free and Equal: Photographs of the Loyal Japanese Americans at Manzanar Relocation Center, Inyo County, California.* New York: United States Camera.

Adams, David Wallace. 1995. *Education for Extinction: American Indians and the Boarding School Experience.* Lawrence: University Press of Kansas.

Alexi, Sherman. 1996. *Indian Killer.* New York: Warner Books.

Allen, Paula Gunn. 1986. *Sacred Hoop: Recovering the Feminine in American Indian Traditions.* Boston: Beacon Press.

Armor, John, and Peter Wright. 1988. *Manzanar: Photographs by Ansel Adams, Commentary by John Hersey.* New York: Vintage Books.

Bahr, Diana Meyers. 1995. *From Mission to Metropolis: Cupeño Indian Women in Los Angeles.* Norman: University of Oklahoma Press.

Bahr, Howard M., Bruce A. Chadwick, and Robert C. Day, eds. 1972. *Native Americans Today: Sociological Perspectives.* New York: Harper and Row.

Bataille, Gretchen M., and Kathleen M. Sands. 1984. *American Indian Women Telling Their Lives.* Lincoln: University of Nebraska Press.

Berg, S. Carol. 1989. Memories of an Indian Boarding School: White Earth, Minnesota, 1909–1945. *Midwest Review* 11 (Spring): 27–36.

Blaeser, Kimberly M. 1997. Like "Reeds Through the Ribs of a Basket": Native Women Weaving Stories. *American Indian Quarterly* 21 (4): 555–65.

Boyer, Ruth McDonald, and Narcissus Duffy Gayton. 1992. *Apache Mothers and Daughters.* Norman: University of Oklahoma Press.

Burgess, Roxanne, and Polly Johnson. 2000. "Native American Ministry, Southern California Style." *Church and Society. Presbyterian Church (U.S.A.).*, March/April.

Burton, Jeffery F., Mary M. Farrell, Florence E. Lord, and Richard W. Lord. 1999. Confinement and Ethnicity: An Overview of World War II Japanese American Relocation Sites. Publications in Anthropology 74. Tucson: Western Archeological and Conservation Center.

Burton, Jeffery F., and Jane C. Wehrey. 1996. History Background. In *Three Farewells to Manzanar: The Archeology of Manzanar Historic Site, California,* edited by Jeffery F. Burton. Publications in Anthropology 67. Tucson: Western Archeological and Conservation Center.

Campbell, Maria. 1973. *Halfbreed.* Lincoln: University of Nebraska Press.

Chalfant, W. A. 1933. *The Story of Inyo.* Bishop, Calif.: Chalfant Press.

Child, Brenda J. 1999. *Boarding School Season: American Indian Families, 1900–1940.* Lincoln: University of Nebraska Press.

Clemmer, Richard O., and Omer C. Stewart. 1986. Treaties, Reservations, and Claims. In *Handbook of North American Indians*. Edited by William C. Sturtevant. Vol. 11, *Great Basin*, edited by Warren L. D'Azevedo. Washington, D.C.: Smithsonian Institution.

Clifford, James. 1986. Introduction: Partial Truths. In *Writing Culture: The Poetics and Politics of Ethnography*, edited by James Clifford and George E. Marcus. Berkeley and Los Angeles: University of California Press.

Clifton, James A., ed. 1989. *Being and Becoming Indian*. Chicago: Dorsey Press.

Cohen, Irene J., Jeffery F. Burton, and Mary M. Farrell. 1996. Japanese American Relocation. In *Three Farewells to Manzanar: The Archeology of Manzanar National Historic Site, California*, edited by Jeffery F. Burton. Publications in Anthropology 67. Tucson: Western Archeological and Conservation Center.

Coleman, Michael C. 1993. *American Indian Children at School, 1850–1930*. Jackson: University Press of Mississippi.

Cook, Sherburne F. 1976a. *The Population of the California Indians, 1769–1970*. Berkeley and Los Angeles: University of California Press.

———. 1976b. Trends in Marriage and Divorce since 1850. In *The Conflict between the California Indian and White Civilization*. Berkeley and Los Angeles: University of California Press.

Cook-Lynn, Elizabeth. 1996. American Indian Intellectuals and the New Indian Story. *American Indian Quarterly* 20 (1): 57–76.

Crow Dog, Mary, and Richard Erdoes. 1990. *Lakota Woman*. New York: Grove Weidenfeld.

Cruickshank, Julie. 1990. *Life Lived Like a Story: Three Yukon Native Elders*. Lincoln: University of Nebraska Press.

DeDecker, Mary. 1966. *Mines of the Eastern Sierra*. Glendale, Calif.: La Siesta Press.

DeVos, George, and Lola Romanucci-Eoss, eds., *Ethnic Identities, Cultural Continuities, and Change*. Chicago: University of Chicago Press.

Dorris, Michael. 1987. "Indians on the Shelf." In *The American Indian and the Problem of History*, edited by Calvin Martin. New York: Oxford University Press.

Drinnon, Richard. 1987. *Keeper of Concentration Camps: Dillon S. Myer and American Racism*. Berkeley and Los Angeles: University of California Press.

Farquhar. Francis. 1969. *History of the Sierra Nevada*. Berkeley and Los Angeles: University of California Press.

Fischer, Michael M. J. 1986. Ethnicity and the Post-Modern Arts of Memory. In *Writing Culture: The Poetics and Politics of Ethnography*, edited by James Clifford and George E. Marcus. Berkeley and Los Angeles: University of California Press.

Fixico, Donald L. 1986. *Termination and Relocation: Federal Indian Policy, 1945–1960.* Albuquerque: University of New Mexico Press.

Forstenzer, Martin. 1993. Plans to Honor Manzanar Create Divided Camps. *Los Angeles Times,* 23 December.

———. 1995. Gambling on a Roadside Attraction. *Los Angeles Times,* 16 November.

———. 1996. Bitter Feelings Still Run Deep at the Camp. *Los Angeles Times,* 4 April.

Garrod, Andrew, and Colleen Larimore, eds. 1997. *First Person, First Peoples: Native American Graduates Tell Their Life Stories.* Ithaca: Cornell University Press.

Haig-Brown, Celia. 1988. *Resistance and Renewal: Surviving the Indian Residential School.* Vancouver, B.C.: Tillacum Library.

Hansen, Arthur A., and Betty E. Mitson, eds. 1974. *Voices Long Silent: An Oral Inquiry into the Japanese-American Evacuation.* Fullerton: California State University, Fullerton, Japanese-American Oral History Project.

Hart, E. Richard. 1986. The Indian Claims Commission. In *Indian Self-Rule: First-Hand Accounts of Indian-White Relations from Roosevelt to Reagan,* edited by Kenneth R. Philp. Salt Lake City: Howe Brothers.

Hertzberg, Hazel W. 1971. *The Search for an American Indian Identity: Modern Pan-Indian Movements.* Syracuse: Syracuse University Press.

Horne, Esther Burnett, and Sally McBeth. 1998. *Essie's Story: The Life and Legacy of a Shoshone Teacher.* Lincoln: University of Nebraska Press.

Hundley, Norris, Jr. 1992. *The Great Thirst: Californians and Water, 1770s–1990s.* Berkeley and Los Angeles: University of California Press.

Ichioka, Yuji, ed. 1989. *Views from Within: The Japanese-American Evacuation and Resettlement Study.* Los Angeles: UCLA Asian American Studies Center.

Kahrl, William L. 1982. *Water and Power: The Conflict over Los Angeles' Water Supply in the Owens Valley.* Berkeley and Los Angeles: University of California Press.

Karst, Kenneth L. 1995. Myths of Identity: Individual and Group Portraits of Race and Sexual Orientation. *UCLA Law Review* 43 (2): 263–369.

Karttuner, Francis E. 1994. *Between Worlds: Interpreters, Guides, and Survivors.* New Brunswick: Rutgers University Press.

Katz, Jane, ed. 1995. *Messengers of the Wind: Native American Women Tell Their Life Stories.* New York: Ballantine Books.

Kelly, Lawrence C. 1988. United States Indian Policies, 1900–1980. In *Handbook of North American Indians*. Edited by William C. Sturtevant. Vol. 4, *History of Indian-White Relations*, edited by Wilcomb E. Washburn. Washington, D.C.: Smithsonian Institution.

Kidwell, Clara Sue. 1986. Education Policy and Graduate Education for American Indian Students. In *American Indian Policy and Cultural Values: Conflict and Accommodation*, edited by Jennie Joe. UCLA: American Indian Studies Center.

———. 1992. Indian Women as Culture Mediators. *Ethnography* 39:97–107.

Knack, Martha C. 1980. *Life Is with People: Household Organizations of Contemporary Southern Paiute Indians*. Anthropology Papers 19. Edited by Lowell John Bean and Thomas C. Blackburn. Socorro, New Mexico: Ballena Press.

———. 1987. The Role of Credit in Native Adaptation to the Great Basin Ranching Economy. *American Indian Culture and Research Journal* 11 (1): 43–65.

Kroeber, A. L. 1976. *Handbook of the Indians of California*. New York: Dover Publications.

Langness, L. L., and Geyla Frank. 1981. *Lives: An Anthropological Approach to Biography*. Novato, Calif.: Chandler and Sharp Publishers.

Liberty, Margot, ed. 1978. *American Indian Intellectuals*. St. Paul: West Publishing.

Liljeblad, Sven, and Catherine S. Fowler. 1986. Owens Valley Paiute. In *Handbook of North American Indians*. Edited by William C. Sturtevant. Vol. 11, *Great Basin*, edited by Warren L. D'Azenedo. Washington, D.C.: Smithsonian Institution.

Lobo, Susan. 1998. Is Urban a Person or a Place? Characteristics of Urban Indian Country. *American Indian Culture and Research Journal* 20 (4): 89–102.

Lomawaima, K. Tsianina. 1993. Domesticity in the Federal Indian Schools: The Power of Authority over Mind and Body. *American Ethnologist* 20 (2): 227–40.

———. 1994. *They Called It Prairie Light: Oral Histories from Chilocco Indian Agricultural School, 1920–1940*. Lincoln: University of Nebraska Press.

Lowry, Annie. 1966. *Karnee: A Paiute Narrative*. Edited by Lalla Scott. Reno: University of Nevada Press.

Mankiller, Wilma, and Michael Wallis. 1994. *Mankiller: A Chief and Her People*. New York: St. Martin's.

Manzanar Committee. 1998. *Reflections in Three Self-Guided Tours of Manzanar*. Los Angeles: Manzanar Committee.

McBeth, Sally. 1983. *Ethnic Identity and the Boarding School Experience of West-Central Oklahoma American Indians*. Washington, D.C.: University Press of America.

McBride, Bunny. 1995. *Molly Spotted Elk: A Penobscot in Paris*. Norman: University of Oklahoma Press.

McFee, Malcolm. 1968. The 150 Percent Man, A Product of Blackfeet Acculturation. *American Anthropologist* 70:1096–1103.

Meriam, Lewis. 1928. *The Problem of Indian Administration*. Baltimore: Johns Hopkins Press.

Mihesuah, Devon A. 1996a. Commonality of Difference: American Indian Women and History. *American Indian Quarterly* 20 (1): 15–27.

———. 1996b. Voices, Interpretations, and the New History. *American Indian Quarterly* 20 (1): 91–108.

Miller, J. R. 1996. *Shingwauk's Vision: A History of Native Residential Schools*. Toronto: University of Toronto Press.

Momaday, N. Scott. 1975. The Man Made of Words. In *Literature of the American Indians: Views and Interpretations*, edited by Abraham Chapman. New York: New American Library.

———. 1976. *The Names: A Memoir*. New York: Harper and Row.

———. 1997. *The Man Made of Words: Essays, Stories, Passages*. New York: St. Martin's Press.

The Mono Lake Schoolhouse Museum. n.d. Lee Vining, Calif.: Mono Lake Historical Society.

Mountain Wolf Woman. 1966. *Mountain Wolf Woman, Sister of Crashing Thunder: The Autobiography of a Winnebago Indian*. Edited by Nancy Oestreich Lurie. Ann Arbor: University of Michigan Press.

Okimoto, Ruth Y. 2001. "Sharing a Desert Home: Life on the Colorado River Indian Reservation, Poston, Arizona, 1942–1945." Special report, *News from Native California*, Berkeley.

"The Owens Irony." 1998. *Los Angeles Times*. 25 July, B7.

Parker, Ian L. 1997. Sheldon Hackney. Starting a Conversation on What It Means to Be American. *Los Angeles Times*, 30 November.

Patterson, Victoria. 1989. "Indian Education: Then and . . . " *News from Native California* 4 (1): 32–34.

Potashin, Richard. Trees That Tell a Story. *Newsletter for Friends of the Eastern California Museum* 13 (1, 2): 1–6

Presbyterian Survey of American Indians in Los Angeles. 1989. *Los Angeles Times*, 25 March.

Prucha, Francis Paul. 1976. *American Indian Policy in Crisis: Christian Reformers and the Indian, 1865–1900*. Norman: University of Oklahoma Press.

———. 1979. *The Churches and the Indian Schools, 1888–1912.* Lincoln: University of Nebraska Press.

———. 1983. *The Great Father: The United States Government and the American Indians.* Vols. 1 and 2. Lincoln: University of Nebraska Press.

———, ed. 1973. *Americanizing the American Indians: Writings by the "Friends of the Indians," 1880–1900.* Lincoln: University of Nebraska Press.

Qoyawayma, Polingaysi [Elizabeth Q. White]. 1964. *No Turning Back: A True Account of a Hopi Girl's Struggle to Bridge the Gap between the World of Her People and the World of the White Man.* As told to Vada F. Carlson. Albuquerque: University of New Mexico Press.

Reyhner, Jon, and Jeanne Eder. 1992. A History of Indian Education. In *Teaching American Indian Students,* edited by Jon Reyhner. Norman: University of Oklahoma Press.

Roosens, Eugene E. 1989. *Creating Ethnicity: The Process of Ethnogenesis.* Frontiers of Anthropology 5. Newbury Park: Sage Publications.

Schumacher, Genny. 1962. *Deepest Valley: Guide to Owens Valley and Its Mountain Lakes, Roadsides, and Trails.* San Francisco: Sierra Club.

Scott, Lalla. 1966. *Karnee: A Paiute Narrative.* Reno: University of Nevada Press.

Shaw, Anna Moore. 1974. *A Pima Past.* Tucson: University of Arizona Press.

Shoemaker, Nancy. 1988. Urban Indians and Ethnic Choices: American Indian Organizations in Minneapolis, 1920–1950. *Western Historical Quarterly* 19 (4): 431–47.

Simmons, Leo W., ed. 1942. *Sun Chief: The Autobiography of a Hopi Indian.* New Haven: Yale University Press.

Smith, Genny, ed., 1993. *Mammoth Lakes Sierra: A Handbook for Roadside and Trail.* Mammoth Lakes, Calif.: Genny Smith Books.

Spence, Mark. Dispossessing the Wilderness: Yosemite Indians and the National Park Ideal, 1864–1930. *Pacific Historical Review* 65 (1): 27–59.

Steward, Julian H., and Erminie Wheeler-Voegelin. 1974. *Paiute Indians III: The Northern Paiute Indians.* New York: Garland.

Stewart, Irene. 1980. *A Voice in Her Tribe: A Navajo Woman's Own Story.* Doris Istrander Dawdy, ed. Socorro, New Mexico: Ballena Press.

Stonequist, Everett V. [1937] 1961. *The Marginal Man: A Study in Personality and Culture Conflict.* New York: Russell and Russell.

Straus, Terry, and Debra Valentino. 1998. Retribalization in Urban Indian Communities. *American Indian Culture and Research Journal* 22 (4): 103–15.

Swan, Madonna. 1991. *Madonna Swan: A Lakota Woman's Story*. As told to Mark St. Pierre. Norman: University of Oklahoma Press.

Swann, Brian, and Arnold Krupat, eds. 1987. *I Tell You Now: Autobiographical Essays by Native American Writers*. Lincoln: University of Nebraska Press.

Szasz, Margaret Connell. 1977. *Education and the American Indian: The Road to Self-determination Since 1928*. Albuquerque: University of New Mexico Press.

———, ed. 1994. *Between Indian and White Worlds*. Norman: University of Oklahoma Press.

Trennert, Robert A., Jr. 1982. Educating Indian Girls at Non-reservation Boarding Schools, 1878–1920. *Western Historical Quarterly* 13:271–90.

———. 1983. Carlisle to Phoenix: The Rise and Fall of the Indian Outing System, 1878–1930. *Pacific Historical Review* 52:267–91.

———. 1988. Victorian Morality and Supervision of Indian Women Working in Phoenix, 1906–1930. *Journal of Social History* 22:113–28.

Udall, Louise, ed. 1969. *Me and Mine: The Life Story of Helen Sekaquaptewa*. Tucson: University of Arizona Press.

Underhill, Ruth. 1941. *The Northern Paiute Indians of California and Nevada*. Lawrence, Kans.: U.S. Office of Education, Indian Affairs, Haskell Institute.

Unrau, Harlan D. 1996. *The Evacuation and Relocation of Persons of Japanese Ancestry during World War II: A Historical Study of the Manzanar War Relocation Center*. Washington, D.C.: U.S. Department of the Interior, National Park Service.

Van Horn, Lawrence F. 1995. *Native American Consultations and Ethnographic Assessment, the Paiutes and Shoshones of Owens Valley, California*. Denver: U.S. Department of the Interior, National Park Service.

The View from Within: Japanese American Art from the Internment Camps, 1942–1945. 1992. Los Angeles: The Japanese American Museum, The UCLA Wight Art Gallery, and the UCLA Asian American Studies Center.

Walter, Nancy Peterson. 1986. The Land Exchange Act of 1937: Creation of the Indian Reservations at Bishop, Big Pine, and Lone Pine, California, through a Land Trade between the United States of America and the City of Los Angeles. Ph.D. diss., Union for Experimenting Colleges, Universities Without Walls, and Union Graduate School, Cincinnati, Ohio.

Walton, John. 1992. *Western Times and Water Wars: State, Culture, and Rebellion in California*. Berkeley and Los Angeles: University of California Press.

Weibel-Orlando, Joan. 1991. *Indian Country L.A.: Maintaining Ethnic Community in Complex Society.* Urbana: University of Illinois Press.

Wheat, Margaret M. 1967. *Survival Arts of the Primitive Paiutes.* Reno: University of Nevada Press.

Witmer, Linda F. 1993. *The Indian Industrial School, Carlisle, Pennsylvania, 1879–1918.* Carlisle: Cumberland County Historical Society.

Young, Mary. 1987. Pagans, Converts, and Backsliders All: A Secular View of the Metaphysics of Indian-White Relations. In *The American Indian and the Problem of History*, edited by Calvin Martin. New York: Oxford University Press.

Index

www.ingramcontent.com/pod-product-compliance
Lightning Source LLC
Chambersburg PA
CBHW022357280326
41935CB00007B/220